AF130755

Bettina Breitenberger

Gawain as the Epitome of Arthurian Knighthood

Lexico-Semantic Differences in the Depiction of Gawain in Middle English and Middle High German

Anchor Academic
Publishing

Breitenberger, Bettina: Gawain as the Epitome of Arthurian Knighthood: Lexico-Semantic Differences in the Depiction of Gawain in Middle English and Middle High German, Hamburg, Anchor Academic Publishing 2015

Buch-ISBN: 978-3-95489-361-4
PDF-eBook-ISBN: 978-3-95489-861-9
Druck/Herstellung: Anchor Academic Publishing, Hamburg, 2015

Bibliografische Information der Deutschen Nationalbibliothek:
Die Deutsche Nationalbibliothek verzeichnet diese Publikation in der Deutschen Nationalbibliografie; detaillierte bibliografische Daten sind im Internet über http://dnb.d-nb.de abrufbar.

Bibliographical Information of the German National Library:
The German National Library lists this publication in the German National Bibliography. Detailed bibliographic data can be found at: http://dnb.d-nb.de

© Anchor Academic Publishing, Imprint der Diplomica Verlag GmbH
Hermannstal 119k, 22119 Hamburg
http://www.diplomica-verlag.de, Hamburg 2015
Printed in Germany

Table of Contents

1. Introduction 7

2. Method 10

    2.1 Choice of Works 10

    2.2 Choice of Word Classes 11

    2.3 Collection of Data 12

    2.4 Evaluation of Data 14

3. Summaries for *Sir Gawain and the Green Knight* and *Parzival* 15

    3.1 *Sir Gawain and the Green Knight* 15

    3.2 *Parzival* 16

4. Gawain in Middle English 17

    4.1 Overview of Expressions in *Sir Gawain and the Green Knight* 17

    4.2 Expressions Used by Gawain 19

    4.3 Expressions Used by Other Characters 21

    4.4 Expressions Used by the Narrator 22

5. Gawain in Middle High German 24

    5.1 Overview of Expressions in *Parzival* 24

    5.2 Expressions Used by Gawain 28

    5.3 Expressions Used by Other Characters 29

    5.4 Expressions Used by the Narrator 31

6. Discussion 34

    6.1 Differences and Similarities in Both Works 34

    6.2 Discussion of the Advantages of a Lexico-Semantic Analysis 35

7. Conclusion 39

Primary Sources 40

Secondary Sources 40

Index of Figures 51

Index of Tables 51

Appendices 52

    I. Complete Data for *Sir Gawain and the Green Knight* 52

    II. Semantic Features in *Sir Gawain and the Green Knight* 57

    III. Complete Data for *Parzival* 61

    IV. Semantic Features in *Parzival* 67

    V. Comparison of Semantic Features 81

1. Introduction

The tales of King Arthur and his Knights of the Round Table have fascinated people throughout the centuries and are still today adapted for books, films and TV series. While Arthur and Merlin are perceived as special characters, the different Knights of the Round Table seem to have faded into a more blurry assemblage of men.

In the Middle Ages, however, Gawain was seen as the perfect Arthurian knight who clearly sets himself apart and embodies the principles and values of the Round Table. "The earlier French romances present [him] as the standard of courtesy and discretion against whom all others are measured" (Thompson/ Busby 2006: 27) and due to French literature being the source for many other Arthurian romances, this image of Gawain can also be found in the works of Middle High German writers as well as Middle English ones. But is Gawain depicted in exactly the same way in those two cultures or do the authors focus on different aspects of his personality? Where are the differences and similarities in the nouns and adjectives used to describe the protagonist? Do some expressions only occur for a distinct user, like the narrator? And additionally, are there nouns and adjectives which only appear before or after a certain event? Considering several aspects (see 2.1 Choice of Works), *Sir Gawain and the Green Knight* by the *Gawain*-Poet and *Parzival* by Wolfram von Eschenbach were selected for analysis.

In research literature, hardly any efforts were made to find an answer to those questions. Regarding *Sir Gawain and the Green Knight*, nouns are only discussed with focus on alliterative verse. So, Turville-Petre argues that alliteration demands a broad variety of synonyms that can be filled into the alliterative scheme (1977: 70), and thus, that the nouns *burne, freke, gome, haþel, lede, renk, schalk, segge* and *wyȝe* (1977: 78) – he misses "tulk" (*SGGK*[1], 18) – for *man* and *warrior* are not distinguishable by their meaning. "[T]he special status of these words is their function and position in the alliterative line" (Turville-Petre 1977: 82). In regard to semantic features, *gome, renk* and *schalk* could indeed be categorized as synonyms as they all determine [WARRIOR]. *Freke*, however, adds the feature [BRAVE] whereas *haþel* and *burne* can be further distinguished by the feature [NOBLE].[2] It is thus rejected here to

---

[1] Sir Gawain and the Green Knight will be shortened to *SGGK* for quotations in the text.
[2] See appendix 'Table 6 - Semantic Features of Nouns in *Sir Gawain and the Green Knight*', page 53.

call those expressions synonyms as they convey not the exact same meaning.

In addition, Turville-Petre deals with the use of nominalized adjectives which, according to him, enable the poet "to draw attention very economically to one particular aspect of the object that he wishes to emphasise" (1977: 81). In contrast to nouns, nominalized adjectives have a "very sharply defined" (1977: 81) meaning and "[t]heir function is to stress the aspect of the character that is relevant to the reader at that point in the poem" (1977: 81).

Alliterative adjectives are analyzed by Marie Borroff. Her focus is on *gode* and *gay* in connection with *Gawain* and will therefore be discussed in section 4.1 of this book.

For *Parzival*, it is Dietrich Homberger's dissertation which offers a detailed characterization of Gawain. The hero's behavior in different situations, his strengths and weaknesses and his relationship with women or God are taken into account. Homberger's findings, however, are only partially based on single expressions due to his more literary approach. Problems occur in regard to his data. On the one hand, for his chapter "Beinamen, Epitheta" (see Homberger 1970: 118), he adds a detailed appendix (Homberger 1970: 236). On the other hand, there is no explanation available why firstly, this chapter is limited to the expressions *degen*, *helt*, *wîgant*, *kurtoys*, *wirt* and *bote* and secondly, why not every occurrence of a word is taken into account. For *kurtois*, which he mentions for lines 380,28 and 619,25 but can also be found in line 619,25, this might just be an error due to eye skip. For *wirt*, however, he mentions only two examples while it actually occurs six times.[3]

In his appendix about adjectives (see Homberger 1970: 238), similar problems exist. Due to the comparison of *Parzival* to other German works, Homberger probably limited his choice of adjectives in order to get the biggest possible overlap. For direct references to Gawain, the adjectives *ahtbære*, *edel*, *liep*, *tum* and *vremde* are missing. On the other hand, his list is extended by adjectives which relate to attributes of Gawain, like "vester mout" (Eschenbach 1961: 571,04) 'unchanging courage'. As Homberger does not indicate any verse lines, it is difficult to follow his results. Moreover, it does not become exactly clear what Homberger draws from his findings in regard to adjectives. Apart from an implication that they would extend Gawain's image and praise for Eschenbach due to his broad variation of adjectives (Homberger 1970: 118), there seem no further insights to be gained for him.

---

[3] See appendix 'Table 9 - Collection of Nouns for *Parzival*', page 57.

While the works mentioned above deal with Gawain in only one particular language, *Gawain: A Casebook* or *The Oxford Guide to Arthurian Literature and Legend* consider his figure in different cultures, especially in English, French, German and Dutch literature. As their focus is on one language at a time, cross linguistic comparisons of Gawain could not be found.

In order to fill this gap, this study will examine the nouns and adjectives used by the *Gawain*-Poet and Eschenbach to characterize their protagonists. It is the aim to determine the differences and similarities in the depiction of Gawain and to discuss possible reasons for certain word choices. The following chapter will therefore describe how the works for this analysis were chosen, why the focus is on nouns and attributive adjectives as well as how and which data was collected. The first half of the main part will start with an overview of the different expressions that were used in the text *Sir Gawain and the Green Knight*. The next part will deal with references Gawain uses for himself, followed by how other characters address and talk about the knight. After that, the narrators' ways to describe the protagonists will be analyzed. The second half of the main part will then be about the same aspects for *Parzival*, followed by a discussion of the differences and similarities of both works. Moreover, it will be dealt with the question whether a lexico-semantic approach offers further insights into the characterization of Gawain. In the conclusion, the findings of this study will be summarized.

2. Method

2.1 Choice of Works

In order to be well comparable, the sources for Middle English and Middle High German should have as many characteristics in common as possible. For the English text, *Sir Gawain and the Green Knight* offers not only the advantage of Gawain being the main character – it is also written in verse. Due to the German sources being all poems, choosing *Sir Gawain and the Green Knight* allows to look for the best possible counterpart in Middle High German literature.

Although *Diu Crône* by Heinrich von dem Türlin also has Gawain as the main hero, he "undergoes neither evolution nor crisis" (Thompson/Busby 2006: 10) and is, in contrast to Gawain in *Sir Gawain and the Green Knight*, already a fixed character. For this reason, Wolfram von Eschenbach's *Parzival* was preferred to *Diu Crône*, despite the fact that Gawain is only the second main character there. Parzival and Gâwân, as he is called in Middle High German, go on different adventures and therefore have their own episodes. This allows seeing Gâwân as the main character in his parts of the story, making *Sir Gawain and the Green Knight* and *Parzival* comparable.

Another important aspect in regard to comparability is the time in which both works occurred. For the manuscript of *Sir Gawain and the Green Knight*, it seems certain that it was created around 1400 (Brewer D. 1997:1 & Bennet 1997:71). However, the manuscript is a transcription of the original poem and it is unknown in which year the actual work was written. While Bennet suggests that it might have been produced "as early as the 1360s or as late as the manuscript itself" (1997:71), Edwards argues that the poem surely existed before the manuscript. Furthermore, he concludes from the inscription "HONY SOYT QUI MAL PENCE" (*SGGK*, 69) that the year 1348 "provides the earliest possible date for the transcription of the manuscript itself" (1997:198). However, he comments that the inscription might not have been "copied at the same time as the text or by the same scribe" (1997:198) and Barron adds that "there is no evidence that the poet himself intended any reference" (1994: 181) to the Garter motto. Moreover, he writes that because of the armor and equipment described in the story it is concluded that the work was written "in the last ten or fifteen years of the fourteenth century" (1994: 25).

In contrast to *Sir Gawain and the Green Knight*, the dating of *Parzival* seems less complicated. In the seventh book of his work, Eschenbach writes about the still bad condition of Erfurt's wine gardens, which were trampled down by horses (Eschenbach 1961: 379,18[4]). According to Bumke, this refers to the siege of Erfurt in the spring of 1203 and he concludes that the smaller part of *Parzival* was written before 1203/1204 (1970: 11). On the other hand, he takes into account that the work might have been edited several times which opens up the possibility that comments like this have been included at a later time. As a result, he dates the poem between 1200 and 1210 (Bumke 1970: 12).

Even if, in conclusion, *Sir Gawain and the Green Knight* and *Parzival* are up to 200 years apart, the two works share a connecting feature. Both of them are influenced by the French writer Chrétien de Troyes. Though Eschenbach's indication of sources is rather unclear, comparisons with Chrétien's *Conte du Graal* showed that his *Perceval* can be seen as *Parzival*'s main source (Bumke 1970: 33).

In her article "The Sources of *Sir Gawain and the Green Knight*", Elizabeth Brewer writes that it would be almost "virtually certain" (1997: 245) that the *Gawain*-Poet was familiar with the episode of the Beheading-game in the *First Continuation* of *Perceval*.

In summary, the aspects of verse, date, source and Gawain being a main character led to the decision that *Sir Gawain and the Green Knight* and *Parzival* were suitable works in order to answer the research question of how the figures' character is presented in Middle English and Middle High German literature.

2.2 Choice of Word Classes

There are four word classes which allow characterizing Gawain: nouns, adjectives, verbs and adverbs. The nouns can be split into two groups. On the one hand, there are nouns which replace the name 'Gawain', like "kniȝt" (*SGGK*, 11) 'knight' or "degen" (Eschenbach 1961: 299,30) 'warrior'. On the other hand, nouns that in some way describe his manner can be found. While it is a rather easy choice to include "kraft" (Eschenbach 1961: 558,22) 'strength' or "honour" (*SGGK*, 34) 'honor', it is difficult to decide what to do with "Your [Gawain's] worde" (*SGGK*, 42). As Gawain's talent for speeches is regularly mentioned, it seems important to be included. Yet, the noun *worde* itself does not transport

---

[4] All quotes from *Parzival* are indicated with 'stanza,verse line' to make them searchable on the TITUS website.

the information that his talks were outstanding or much appreciated by others. Due to this problematic differentiation, only those types of nouns which replace Gawain's name were taken into account. Consequently, only the attributive adjectives that refer to Gawain or the according replacement expressions were collected for the data.

For verbs, it would be necessary to find rules by which expressions are accepted into the corpus. Otherwise, the amount of verbs like *say* or *go* and their conjugated forms that are used to describe basic actions but do not have a greater meaning for Gawain's character would be too high. However, as Gawain's talent for speech is a characteristic of him, verbs that express the idea of saying something are important to be added. Here, the problem arises to decide which verbs have more meaning for the protagonist's character than others.

To limit the amount of verbs accepted into the corpus, it would also be possible, for example, to distinguish between verbs that describe an activity or a state. At first glance, one might decide to collect only activity verbs as people can be well characterized by their actions. On the other hand, for *Gawain and the Green Knight*, the significance of Gawain staying in bed all day while his host is on a hunt cannot be denied. Consequently, one can conclude that state verbs can also be important for analysis. Again, the question arises on how to determine verbs that are significant for the depiction of Gawain's character and, thus, need to be added to the corpus. For this reason, the focus will be on adjectives and on nouns as described above.

2.3 Collection of Data

In a first approach, both texts were read in order to collect a basis of nouns and adjectives as well as declined forms which are used to refer to Gawain. Especially for the Middle English text, attention was paid to alternative forms of spelling. In a second approach, search functions were used to assure a complete collection of data.

Nouns like the Middle English *sir* and the Middle High German *her*, which are used by the narrator and in direct speech to address Gawain, were not taken into account as they only stress the protagonist's nobility or are a formal form of politeness and respect, but do not add further characteristics to the concept of Gawain.

Plural forms were included when a direct reference to Gawain existed. In "There gode Gawan watz grayþed Gwenore bisyde,/And Agrauayn a la dure mayn on þat oþer syde sittes,/Boþe þe kynges sistersunes and ful siker kniȝtes" (*SGGK*, 4) 'There, good Gawain was seated next to Guinevere, and Agravain with the hard hand sits on the other side – both the king's sister's sons and very doughty knights', for example, it is clear that *sistersunes* and *kniȝtes* refer to 'Gawain and Agravain' due to their mentioning two verse lines before and were thus added to the data. General references to knights or else, however, where Gawain might possibly – but not for sure – be part of, were omitted. This, of course, accounts for the Middle High German text as well.

Nouns and adjectives used in sentences with a conjunctive verb form were only taken into account, when the conjunctive's function was to indicate indirect speech. If, however, it was used to signalize a possibility for Gawain to be or become, for example, a coward due to his actions, it was not included as it did not express a fact in the present of the story. The same accounts for nouns and adjectives that occurred in a negated sentence.

All collected terms were extended by user information. Those which were mentioned by the narrator were marked with 'N', those used by Gawain to refer to himself were labeled with 'G' and those which were brought up by minor characters were marked with 'O' for 'others', together with the character's name if available. Being able to sort nouns and adjectives by those parameters offers the possibility to discover if certain expressions are limited to particular users only.

The indication of verse lines enables to determine whether nouns or adjectives are connected to distinct events in the story and do only appear before or after them.

All expressions were assigned to three different groups: Adjectives, Nouns and Appositions. As the two categories 'Nouns' and 'Appositions' overlap, the differences between them will be explained in the following.

An apposition is seen as "a noun phrase immediately after another noun phrase that refers to the same person" (OAAD) and in the context of this study, to Gawain. Though it is not restrictive, the apposition is not separated with a comma. All expressions categorized as an apposition follow the scheme 'Gawain' + 'article' + 'nominalized adjective/noun', e.g. "Gawayn þe gode" (*SGGK*, 31) 'Gawain the Good' or "Gâwân der wirt" (Eschenbach 1961: 764,08) 'Gawain the Host'. An exception to this rule is the Middle High German "von

Norwæge Gâwân" (Eschenbach 1961: 651,10), where the apposition precedes the name due to the less strict syntax. Relative clauses like "Gâwân der ellenthafte degen" (Eschenbach 1961: 418,03) 'Gawain, the brave warrior' were split up into adjective and noun.

2.4 Evaluation of Data

To find out which characteristics of Gawain were especially important for the authors and to make these findings comparable, one has to take a look at the semantic features of the expressions. For this, dictionaries were consulted and the definitions given were used to determine the semantic features. As nouns can have different meanings according to their use, the context of each expression was considered to ensure a thorough evaluation. In case of the Middle High German *gast*, for example, a differentiation was made between its meanings 'guest' and 'stranger'.

In the next step, every semantic feature of a noun or adjective was multiplied by the word's number of occurrences in the text. The result allows to determine which aspects of Gawain are predominant in the work examined. To contrast *Sir Gawain and the Green Knight* with *Parzival*, the results' percentage for the total of semantic features was calculated respectively[5].

Redundant semantic features like [HUMAN], [MALE], [ADULT] were not added to concentrate on the more defining aspects of the protagonist. This, in turn, automatically leads to words like *man* having no relevant semantic features. To avoid that such words drop out of the analysis, they will be discussed independently and added to statistics as *neutral expressions*.

The term *reference* is used to describe the way characters express their thoughts about the protagonist and is not used with its pragmatic meaning.

---

[5] See appendix 'Figure 5 - Distribution of Semantic Features in Percent', page 77.

3. Summaries for *Sir Gawain and the Green Knight* and *Parzival*

In order to understand the differences in regard to the characterization of Gawain in both works, it is important to know the context in which both interact. Therefore, the following abstracts will provide a brief overview of the two plots.

3.1 *Sir Gawain and the Green Knight*

Celebrating Christmas at Arthur's court, the court society is interrupted by the Green Knight, who demands a Christmas game: a member of the Knights of the Round Table shall hit him with his axe but will receive a blow in return after one year. It is Gawain, who in the end accepts the challenge and beheads the Green Knight. Still alive, the stranger demands Gawain to keep his word and to meet him at the Green Chapel in a year's time.

When the set date comes near, Gawain leaves Arthur's court to look for the Green Chapel. On his way, he comes to Bertilak's castle and is welcomed as a guest. The lord and the knight agree to exchange every evening what the host achieves during a hunt while Gawain will give him everything he receives at the castle.

Three days in a row, Bertilak's wife comes to Gawain's chamber and kisses him, but on the third day also gives him a green girdle, which has the power to protect from death. While the protagonist exchanges the kisses for the hunting trophies, he keeps the green girdle to protect himself because he has to face the fight against the Green Knight the next day.

When arriving at the Green Chapel, the Green Knight fakes two blows but cuts Gawain's neck with a third. He then reveals that he is Bertilak and that Gawain has received the cut for keeping the girdle, which was against their agreement. Full of shame, Gawain returns to Arthur's court, wearing the girdle as a visible sign for his fault.

3.2 *Parzival*

In *Parzival*, Gawain occurs rather late in the story. In the presence of Arthur's court, he is accused by Kingrimursel of killing someone without reason and is thus asked to come to Schampfanzun to solve the matter by a fight.

On his way, Gawain passes a castle, which is under attack because the daughter of the castle's lord rejected King Meljanz' love. Gawain is able to settle the dispute between the couple and moves on.

In Schampfanzun, he is seen kissing King Vergulaht's sister which results in a fight between him and the king's men. The knight is supported by Kingrimursel, who had guaranteed Gawain would be safe before their fight. The matter can be settled when the protagonist agrees to take over Vergulaht's task to search for the Holy Grail.

Travelling further, he meets the lady Orgelûse and instantly falls in love with her. She rejects him, but Gawain does not give up. Thus, she grabs the opportunity when she gets the chance to leave him behind, but allows him to see her again if he wins a fight against a certain knight. In the course of this task, Gawain learns about an enchanted castle where noble ladies are held captive. He is the first to survive the adventures in the castle and as a result becomes lord of it. Orgelûse meets Gawain again and gets healed from her bitterness when the hero declares to fight King Gramoflanz, the murderer of Orgelûse's husband. The twist here is that Gramoflanz is the love of Gawain's sister and in case of a fight, Itonjê would either lose her beloved or her brother. Artus thus intervenes and both couples get married.

4. Gawain in Middle English

In the following chapters, the different findings of the analysis will be presented and discussed. There will be a detailed look onto the users of certain expressions and terms related to a distinct event, but for a start, a general overview of the expressions for the Middle English work will be given.

4.1 Overview of Expressions in *Sir Gawain and the Green Knight*

In total, 210 expressions were found referring to the hero in *Sir Gawain and the Green Knight*.[6] The biggest group is formed by nouns, making up 173 words, followed by 32 adjectives and 5 appositions.

For nouns, 24 different terms can be found referring to Gawain. The most frequent ones, which occur more than 10 times, are represented in Figure 1 below.

Figure 1 - Most Frequent Nouns for *Sir Gawain and the Green Knight*

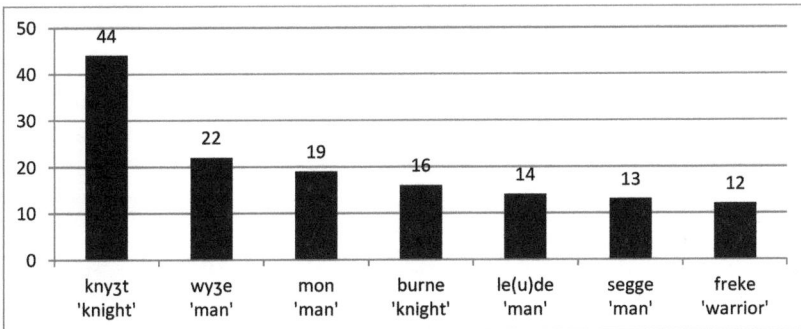

Freke is followed by *haþel* 'warrior' (6 times), *prynce* 'prince' (6), *renk* 'soldier' (4), *hende* 'courtly' (3), *dere* 'dear' (2) and – one time respectively – by *comly* 'handsome', *cosyn* 'cousin', *feble* '(mentally) weak', *gome* 'warrior', *ientyle* 'gentle', *noble* 'noble', *schalk* 'warrior', *stalworth* 'strong', *tulk* 'soldier', *wlonk* 'noble', *wok* 'weak' and *sistersun* 'sister's son'.

While there is quite a variety of different terms, their frequency is quickly descending. This is similar for the group of adjectives. Here, *gode* 'good' is the most frequent expression with 7 occurrences, followed by *bolde* 'brave' and *comli* 'handsome' with 3. The adjectives *fre* 'noble', *gentyle* 'gentle', *hende* 'courtly', *luflych* 'lovely', and *stif* 'strong' can be found two times each, while *derf*

---

[6] See appendix 'I. Complete Data for *Sir Gawain and the Green Knight'*, page 48.

'brave', *fautles* 'faultless', *gay* 'cheerful', *myry* 'cheerful', *noble* 'noble', *siker* 'doughty', *trwe* 'loyal', *welcome* 'welcome' and *vnworþy* 'unworthy' occur only once. For appositions, the phrases *þe gode* 'the good' (2 times), *þe hende* 'the courtly' (1), *þe noble* 'the noble' (1) and *þe blyþe* 'the joyful' (1) could be found.

When semantic features are assigned to these expressions[7], it becomes apparent that his noble descent and being a fighter are the most important aspects of Gawain's character and define him most (see Table 1). They set the basis for a further enhancement of qualities: the features of bravery and strength add more detail to his knighthood and his power corresponds with his aristocratic and royal status in society.

Table 1 - Distribution of Semantic Features in *SGGK*

	Nouns	Adjectives	Appositions	Total
[NOBLE]	80	11	2	93
[WARRIOR]	91	0	0	91
[BRAVE]	19	8	2	29
[POWERFUL]	9	5	1	15
[HANDSOME]	4	9	0	13
[POLITE]	4	4	1	9
[GOOD]	0	7	2	9
[STRONG]	1	3	0	4
[CHEERFUL]	0	2	1	3
[KIND]	1	2	0	3
[RELATIVE]	2	0	0	2
[DEAR]	2	0	0	2
[WEAK]	2	0	0	2
[LOYAL]	0	1	0	1
[WELCOME]	0	1	0	1
[UNWORTHY]	0	1	0	1
[FAULTLESS]	0	1	0	1

Another important feature is Gawain's goodness, indicated by the adjective *gode*. It occurs frequently in combination with the protagonist's name: *gode Gawain*. The alliteration strengthens this aspect in such a way that Borroff claims it becomes almost redundant (1996: 125). The goodness of Gawain "'goes without saying' [and] can be 'taken for granted'" (Borroff 1996: 125) as she describes it. It is strengthened even more by the protagonist's impeccable manners, a semantic component expressed by the adjective *fautles*.

---

[7] See appendix 'II. Semantic Features in *Sir Gawain and the Green Knight*', page 53.

In regard to his relationship with others, the hero is ascribed the semantic features of politeness, kindness and loyalty. He seems to be a rather cheerful man and the fact that he is good looking is also expressed several times. Being such a pleasant person, minor characters welcome Gawain and hold him dear.

Though the most frequent features deal to a large extend with the hero's social position as a warrior and nobleman and focus less on his contact with others, in general, these entire features picture a protagonist with ideal knightly qualities. It is thus striking to also find the semantic features [WEAK] and [UNWORTHY] which seem to completely stand in contrast to the other characteristics. They are even more noteworthy because it is Gawain himself who uses the corresponding expressions – *the wakkest* and *vnworþy* – to refer to himself. The following chapter will therefore deal with the analysis of expressions the hero uses for himself.

4.2 Expressions Used by Gawain

When the Green Knight enters Arthur's court and asks for someone to challenge him in a Christmas game, no one volunteers and the king is so embarrassed that he offers to strike the blow demanded himself. It is Gawain then, who decides to stand in Arthur's place and reasons it with: "I am *þe wakkest*, I wot, and of wyt *feblest*,/ […] Bot for as much as ȝe ar myn em I am only to prayse" [emphasis mine] (*SGGK*, 10) 'I know, I am the weakest and have the weakest mind. I am only praised because you are my uncle.' He stresses both his physical and mental lack of strength and argues that the only reason for being regarded as a respectable person is due to his kinship with Arthur. The way the narrator describes Gawain, however, is totally different: "Gawan watz for gode knawen, and as golde pured,/Voyded of vche vylany, wyth vertuez ennourned/in mote" (*SGGK*, 18) 'Gawain was known to be good and to be like purified gold, free from all imperfection, equipped with values in heart'. This is not a description suitable for any ordinary Knight of the Round Table but an outstanding member. Yet, the hero does not regard himself as such a man but sees himself as quite the contrary. Being told otherwise, he even actively refuses to accept the ascribed features, as the following example shows.

When Bertilak's wife tells him "Þat alle þe worlde worchipez quere-so ȝe ride;/Your honour, your hendelayk is hendely praysed/ With lordez, wyth ladyes, with alle þat lyf bere." (*SGGK*, 34) 'that the whole world worships you wherever you ride; your honor, your courtliness are nobly praised by the lords, the ladies and everyone who lives there', he vehemently denies being the man she talks about and even adds: "To reche to such reuerence as ȝe reherce here/I am *wyȝe vnworþy*" [emphasis mine] (*SGGK*, 35) ('I am unworthy to receive such respect as you describe here'). Again, the image Gawain has of himself is strangely at odds with the way others perceive him. Regarding the nouns he uses to refer to himself, he also seems to have no interest in stressing his nobility and takes a rather neutral stance towards his social status.[8]

In contrast to the previous examples, the protagonist nevertheless uses a positively connoted adjective as well. When Gawain reaches the Green Chapel and finds no one there, he shouts: "Who stiȝtlez in þis sted me steuen to holde?/For now is *gode* Gawayn goande ryȝt here." [emphasis mine] (*SGGK*, 62) 'Who rules this place to hold a meeting with me? Because now, good Gawain has come right here'. It can be doubted that Gawain mentioned the adjective because he actually regards himself as being good and wants to add this aspect when introducing himself. *Gode* is also not used to distinct himself from another, probably bad, Gawain, as his name alone is enough to make unmistakably clear who he is (cp. *SGGK*, 11). Moreover, the Green Knight expects only one person called Gawain to show up at the chapel that day. Therefore, *gode* is – when regarded as an official enhancement of his name – superfluous in this scene. When translating Gawain's words, Barron encountered the same problem and chose to change it to "Gawain, true to his word" (1994: 149). While it is very well possible that *gode* is meant in that way, it would mean a rather ironic twist for the protagonist's character. Though Gawain might be good in the sense of 'keeping his word', he is nevertheless cheating in a game that was meant to be equal for both participants: he is wearing the green girdle in order to protect himself from death. Accordingly, Gawain would use his excellent reputation to knowingly cover his unfair action. Judging from how downcast and ashamed he is, when the Green Knight reveals to him that he got only cut because of his cheating, it seems rather unlikely that Gawain wanted to put special emphasis on how good he is while knowing he actually is not. That is why it is argued here that *gode* is not used in the sense suggested by Barron, but is rather a redundant addition to his name. This claim is also supported by Gawain's distinctive habit to understate himself, as seen in the analysis of *wakkest, feblest* and *vnworþy*.

---

[8] Compare appendix 'Table 3 - Collection of Nouns for *Sir Gawain and the Green Knight*', page 48 (User 'G') and 'Table 6 - Semantic Features of Nouns in *Sir Gawain and the Green Knight*', page 53.

4.3 Expressions Used by Other Characters

The self-image and the way other people perceive a person often differ. This is also the case for Gawain. The analysis of the expressions he used for himself has shown that the hero tends to understate himself and the evidence that other figures do not share his view could also be found. In the following abstract, it will be looked into how minor characters express this different stance and what features they convey with the nouns and adjectives they use. However, for the Middle English work, only few references could be found.

The usage of the nominalized adjective *hende* is especially characteristic of Lord Bertilak's wife. It contains the semantic features [NOBLE], [POWERFUL], [BRAVE] and [HANDSOME] and is used as a polite form of address (cp. *SGGK*, 35). One time, is even enhanced with "of hyȝe honours" (SGGk, 50) 'of high honors'. While *hende* implies not only nobility and bravery, it also contains the meaning of handsomeness, which offers an explanation why this expression is so predominant for the lady. Gawain's attractiveness is of great significance to her which becomes especially apparent when she refers to him with the superlative form of the adjective *comly*. She calls him the 'most handsome knight' of his time (cp. *SGGK*, 42). This is not only her subjective view, as will become clear when analyzing the expressions the narrator uses.

For the lady's husband, other features of the protagonist are of importance. What the hero says about himself clearly shows a downgrading of his person even before Lord Bertilak reveals that he knows about Gawain keeping the girdle. This aberration, however, does not keep Bertilak from addressing the protagonist as "[b]olde burne" (*SGGK*, 64) 'brave warrior', though not everyone might consider using a girdle to stay alive to be a brave action. Therefore, one might think this to be mere politeness but the Green Knight proofs this thought to be wrong: he tells Gawain that he was the "þe *fautlest* freke þat euer on fote ȝede" [emphasis mine] (*SGGK*, 65) 'most faultless warrior who ever walked on earth', though he admitted he had cut the knight for not exchanging the girdle and hence, for not being without fault. The status he ascribes to Gawain is thus a fixed fact. This feature cannot be changed by any event or action and is similar to the protagonist's goodness.

For King Arthur, the usage of *cosyn*, here 'nephew', could be found (cp. *SGGK*, 11). It is the only time this term occurs and the sole occasion in which another character mentions the relationship between the hero and himself. It can thus be concluded, that kinship is not that important for Gawain's image.

4.4 Expressions Used by the Narrator

While minor characters and the protagonist have only little influence on the general image of the hero due to the rather few occasions for their direct speeches in the story, the narrator takes over a major part in shaping the concept of his main figure.

The most frequent terms referring to Gawain mirror the distribution of nouns in general with slight changes in their order (see Figure 2). They are also used by Gawain and the other characters and especially focus on the features [WARRIOR], [NOBLE] and [BRAVE]: *knyȝt, burne, freke* and *haþel*. It becomes apparent here that it is especially the narrator's credit that being a fighter and nobility are such predominant features of Gawain's character. These aspects are further stressed by the according semantic features of the adjectives *fre*, *gentyle*, *hende*, *derf*, *noble* and *stif*. Nevertheless, the narrator completes his vocabulary with neutral expressions like *mon*, *wyȝe*, *segge* and *lede* as well.

Figure 2 – Distribution of Nouns Used by the Narrator in *Sir Gawain and the Green Knight*[9]

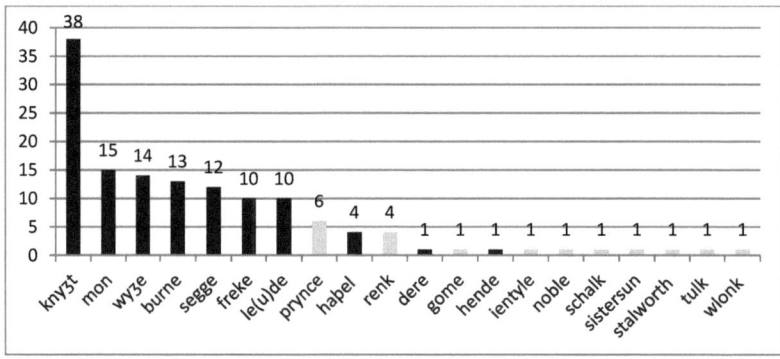

Expressions which are exclusively used by the narrator might offer further characteristics. Those are *prynce* 'prince', *noble* 'noble', *sistersun* 'sister's son', the nominalized adjectives *ientyle* 'gentle', *wlonk* 'noble', *stalworth* 'strong' and those nouns which denote 'warrior': *renk*, *gome*, *schalk*, and *tulk*. For the biggest part, they simply strengthen the already established features described

---

[9] Expressions exclusively used by the narrator are marked with gray.

above. However, they also contribute to a more detailed portray of the protagonist as they ascribe him the features of strength and power.

Sistersun, moreover, is the second mentioning of a noun which refers to the relationship between the main hero and a minor character. Concluding from such rare occurrences, kinship is not only of little importance in the world of the story but also in the world of the reader. Contrary to Gawain's claim that he was only a respected member of the Round Table because of Arthur being his uncle (cp. *SGGK*, 10), family relations are not a major aspect which defines a person.

The protagonist's attractiveness, which was already mentioned by Lord Bertilak's wife, is expressed by the narrator as well. *Hende* occurs both as adjective and nominalized adjective and is even used as an apposition. Its feature [HANDSOME] is further supported by the adjective *comly*. This time, it is the narrator who refers to the hero's good looks, which adds objectivity to the lady's statement.

Another important aspect is Gawain's goodness, which is almost entirely conveyed by the narrator through the adjective *gode*. That this characteristic is not to be doubted becomes obvious when taking the corresponding apposition into account. When talking about "Sir Gawayn þe gode" (SGGK, 53) 'Sir Gawain the Good', the feature [GOOD] is emphasized in a very particular way: it is inseparably linked with the protagonist's name.

The narrator also extends Gawain's characteristics with social skills like politeness and kindness with sporadically occurring adjectives and displays him as a cheerful man, which is also stressed by the apposition *þe blyþe* 'the happy/joyful'.

In conclusion, the Middle English Gawain is to a large extent defined by nobility, fighting skills and knightly manners. For the narrator and minor characters, his goodness and faultlessness are a matter of fact and though it is unknown how the hero accomplished this status, it seems impossible for him to lose it. Interestingly, the protagonist rejects this unique role others assign to him and downgrades himself.

5. Gawain in Middle High German

After the adjectives and nouns for the Middle English Gawain have been analyzed, the focus will now be on the protagonist of the Middle High German work. For a start, there will – like in the previous section – be an overview of the expressions that could be found before taking a closer look onto terms of Gawain, minor characters and the narrator. Afterwards, the findings of this study will be compared to characterizations of Gawain deriving from a less specific approach.

5.1 Overview of Expressions in *Parzival*

For Eschenbach's *Parzival*, 267 expressions were found in total.[10] Here as well, the biggest group is formed by nouns with 180 words, followed by 74 adjectives and 13 appositions. At first glance, in regard to nouns, it seems surprising to find only a slightly higher number in *Parzival* compared to *Sir Gawain and the Green Knight* (172 expressions), though the work is significantly longer. The reason for this is that Eschenbach makes greater use of Gawain's name. While the higher numbers of adjectives can be ascribed to the greater length of the work, the higher amount of appositions might just be a preference of style.

Another difference in regard to both works can be found in the variety of expressions. In *Parzival*, there are 35 different nouns, 27 adjectives and 8 appositions, compared to 23 nouns, 17 adjectives and only 4 different appositions in *Sir Gawain and the Green Knight*.

Interestingly, the most frequently used expression for Gawain is the neutral *man* 'man' (see Figure 3), followed by *gast* (11 times with the meaning 'guest'; 9 times with the meaning 'stranger') *Lôtes sun/ Lôtes kint* 'Lôt's son/Lôt's child' and *neve* 'nephew'. The terms *ritter* 'knight', *helt* 'hero' and *degen* 'warrior', which describe the protagonist's nobility and knighthood, occur rather late. Then, the focus is again on relationships to others which are expressed by *bruoder* 'brother', *swester sun* 'sister's sun' (8 times) and *geselle* ('beloved' 4 times, 'friend' 1 time).

---

[10] See appendix 'III. Complete Data for *Parzival*', page 57.

Figure 3 - Most Frequent Nouns for *Parzival*

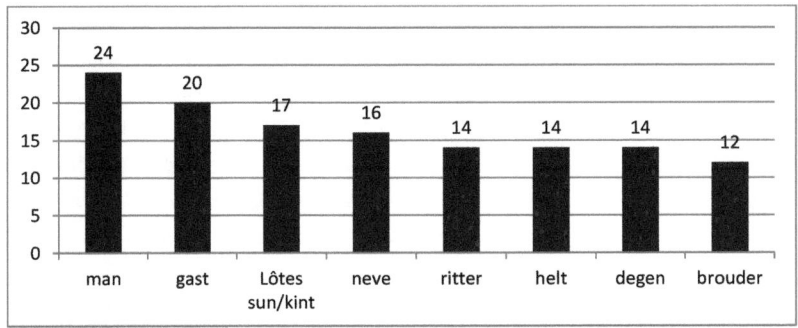

The other nouns used to describe Gawain are *wirt* (5) 'host', *wîgant* 'warrior' (3), *vriunt* 'friend' (2), *bote* 'messenger' (2), *amîs* 'beloved' (1), *stolze* 'proud' (1), *werde* 'noble' (1), *bruodersun* 'brother's son'(1), *minne gernde* 'love longing' (1), *manlîche* 'brave' (1), *prîs* 'glory' (1), *meister* 'teacher' (1), *zil* 'aim' (1), *ellens rîche* 'rich in courage' (1) *êren rîche* 'rich in honors' (1) and *lasters arm* 'poor in shame' (1). Of these, only *wîgant* carries the semantic feature [warrior][11]. It therefore becomes already apparent that in *Parzival*, the protagonist is depicted from a different perspective as in the Middle English counterpart. Moreover, Gawain is accused of being a *trügenære* 'defrauder' (1), a *valschære* 'forger' (2) and a *wehselære* 'money lender' (1). He is insulted as a *gans* 'goose' (2) and a *tumbe* 'dumb man' (1) and – with the same intention – referred to as *koufman* 'trader' (2), *garzun* 'squire' (1) and *arzet* 'Barber-surgeon' (3).

In regard to adjectives, however, only respectable aspects are stressed again – with the exception of *tumm* 'dumb' occurring once. What *gode Gawain* is in Middle English, *werde Gâwân* is in Middle High German. *Wert* 'noble' is the most frequently used adjective with a number of 30 occurrences, followed – with a huge gap – by *balt* 'brave' und *wol geborn* 'of noble birth', which could be found 4 times each. *Hövesch* 'courtly' and *vremd* 'strange (in the sense of 'not familiar to someone)' occur 3 times, while *ellens rich* 'rich in strengh', *manlîch* 'brave', *snel* 'quick', *stolz* 'proud', *unverzaget* 'undismayed', *werlîch* 'able to defend oneself', *(ge)triuwe* 'loyal' and *minne gernde* 'love longing' can be found only twice. There is also a large number of adjectives which exist only once: *ahtbære* 'respected', *edel* 'noble', *ellenthaft* 'couragous', *kamphbære* 'having the

---

[11] See appendix 'Table 13 - Semantic Features of Adjectives in *Parzival*', page 70.

ability to fight', *milte* 'gracious', *starc* 'strong', *tumm* 'dumb', *liep* 'dear', *gezimieret* 'handsome', *hôch* 'big', *süeze* 'friendly', *wol gelobet* 'highly praised', *wol gevar* 'good looking' and *vil guoter* 'very good'.

For appositions, the focus is especially on *der ellens rîche* 'rich in courage' (4 times), followed by *der kurtois* 'the courtly' (3). *Der wirt* 'the host', *der prîses erkande* 'known for glory', *der sælden rîche* 'rich in grace', *der reht gemuote* 'with courtly mind', *der valsches vrîe* 'free of faults' and *von Norwæge* 'of Norway' can be found only once. The latter, however, precedes *Gâwân* due to less strict grammatical orders in Middle High German.

Assigning semantic features to these expressions[12], the focus in relation to Gawain's character is clearly on his kinship to his uncle King Artus, his father King Lôt, his brother and sister as well as his remote relative Parzival and his noble descent which corresponds with his courtly behavior, is almost exclusively expressed by adjectives (see Table 2). His nationality is, different to what one might expect, Norwegian.

The hero's second most important attribute is being a warrior, which is enhanced by aspects like bravery, fearlessness and strength. This, in return, results in depicting him as a glorious but gracious hero, who is even ascribed the feature of faultlessness.

Looking into his interactions with others, he is not only a friend but can also fill the role of a beloved. Concerning the latter, he is described several times as longing for love. He is well respected by others and though the protagonist is often illustrated as a stranger, he is nevertheless welcomed as a guest or is a host for others.

Regarding those main features, the focus is clearly on Gawain's descent. However, it is mostly defined through the kinship to others and thus offers more precise information than the term *nobility* could convey.

---

[12] See appendix 'IV. Semantic Features in *Parzival*', page 63.

Table 2 - Distribution of Semantic Features in *Parzival*

	Nouns	Adjectives	Appositions	Total
[RELATIVE]	57	0	0	57
[WARRIOR]	40	3	0	43
[NOBLE]	1	38	0	39
[COURTLY]	1	33	4	38
[RESPECTED]	1	32	0	33
[HERO]	31	0	0	31
[BRAVE]	16	11	4	31
[STRANGER]	9	3	0	12
[GUEST]	11	0	0	11
[HOST]	5	0	1	6
[BELOVED]	5	0	0	5
[FRIEND]	3	0	0	3
[PROUD]	1	2	0	3
[BARBER-SURGEON]	3	0	0	3
[LOVE LONGING]	1	2	0	3
[GLORIOUS]	2	0	1	3
[GRACIOUS]	0	2	1	3
[QUICK]	0	2	0	2
[UNDISMAYED]	0	2	0	2
[LOYAL]	0	2	0	2
[DUMB]	1	1	0	2
[HANDSOME]	0	2	0	2
[NORWEGIAN]	0	0	2	2
[MESSENGER]	2	0	0	2
[FORGER]	2	0	0	2
[TRADER]	2	0	0	2
[FAULTLESS]	1	0	1	2
[DEFRAUDER]	1	0	0	1
[STRONG]	0	1	0	1
[DEAR]	0	1	0	1
[KIND]	0	1	0	1
[GOOD]	0	1	0	1
[TEACHER]	1	0	0	1
[AIM]	1	0	0	1
[MONEY LENDER]	1	0	0	1
[SQUIRE]	1	0	0	1

5.2 Expressions Used by Gawain

For the Middle High German Gawain, it is difficult to determine the hero's self-image, as there are only few instances in *Parzival* in which the protagonist refers to himself.[13]

In the first example, Gâwân broke off a twig as a love token for Orgelûse. To do so, however, he had entered the property of King Gramoflanz, who encounters him just after the theft. The king explains that he lives to the strict rule to never fight a single man and asks the protagonist to therefore be his messenger and bring a ring to his love Itonjê (Gawain's sister). The hero answers this request with the indignant reply: "ich bin doch *werlîch* ein *man*." [emphasis mine] (Eschenbach, 1961: 607,24) ('I am a man, who is able to defend himself'). This statement shows that Gâwân is well aware of what he is capable of and does not hesitate to express it when it seems necessary to him.

Though the protagonist does not approve of Gramoflanz' treatment, Gâwân nevertheless agrees to be his "bote" (Eschenbach, 1961: 608,01) 'messenger', to bring Itonjê the ring and tell her of the king's love. In the course of their conversation, however, Gramoflanz mentions that his father was killed by the protagonist's father, not knowing that he was tricked to believe so. As King Lôt has died, it is now Gawain whom he seeks for revenge. For this reason, the hero reveals his identity and both men agree to solve the matter by a fight in a few days. This turn of events does not make Gawain change his mind about the promise to deliver the ring to his sister. Neither the feeling of having been insulted nor the wrong accusation against his father seems reason enough to break his word. Though it is only for a limited period of time, he decides to serve a man who might be considered his opponent.

As the kinship to others is in general of high importance, it is not surprising to find Gawain defining himself through his relationship to others. When Antikonîe meets the hero for the first time, she rejects his love ambitions because she does not know him. The protagonist thus quickly explains that he is his "basen bruodersun" (Eschenbach 1961: 406,15) 'the son of his paternal aunt's brother'. Yet, the question arises of what help this information is as Antikonîe knows neither who Gawain is nor who his father and aunt are. It thus appears to be a rather ironic remark.

---

[13] See appendix 'IV. Semantic Features in *Parzival*', page 63.

As far as any conclusions can be drawn from so few occurrences, the Middle High German Gawain on the one hand is more confident of himself. On the other hand, he seems to differentiate between personal and professional matters. While he rejects being seen as an insufficient combatant, he does not react with personal feelings to affairs that come with his profession as a knight.

In general he tends to use nouns which express only a temporary status in consideration of the given circumstances, like *gast* (cp. Eschenbach, 1961: 340,22) or *bote*. This results in his whole character appearing less static: he adapts to his surroundings.

5.3 Expressions Used by Other Characters

In the following, the previously analyzed self-perception of the protagonist will be compared to statements and expressions other characters use to refer to Gawain. While self-references are rare in *Parzival*, a lot more minor characters express how they perceive the hero. One reason for this is the higher number of relatives who play an active part in the story. There is King Artus, who calls Gâwân his *neve* 'nephew' (Eschenbach 1961: 677,08) and his *swestersun* 'sister's son' (Eschenbach 1961: 649,13), and there are also Bêâcurs and Itonjê, the hero's brother and sister, who both stress their kinship with the noun *bruoder* 'brother' (Eschenbach 1961: 323,16 and 711,18). However, the relationship between those four is not only expressed by themselves. Servants as well talk about their master's sister's son (cp. Eschenbach 1961: 684,03) or their mistress' brother (cp. Eschenbach 1961: 697,07) and thus convey or emphasize the importance of kinship.

Characters, which encounter Gawain in the course of the story, usually treat him very respectfully. Though they frequently express by adjectives that he is a stranger to them, he is often referred to their *gast* 'guest' and they talk politely about him being a knight (cp. Eschenbach 1961: 642,15).

Especially the queen Arnîve uses the noun *helt* 'hero' several times, since Gâwân was the only knight ever to survive the tasks at Marveile, a castle under a spell which kept noble women, including herself, captive.[14] As a result, he also resembles their "vreuden zil" (Eschenbach, 1961: 582,20), the reason for their happiness.

Characters who accuse the protagonist of a crime and demand revenge are still polite. Kingrimursel, for example, claims that Gawain killed someone

---

[14] See appendix 'III. Complete Data for *Parzival*', page 58.

without reason and wants to challenge him in a joust. They agree to meet at a certain place and Gawain is guaranteed a save journey. However, the protagonist is involved in a fight with King Vergulaht. This is the moment in which Kingrimursel intervenes: he addresses Gawain as "helt" (Eschenbach 1961: 411,19) and offers him to fight with him against his king.

In contrast to the Middle English Gawain, the Middle High German hero is repeatedly confronted with insults right from the beginning of his journey. Lippaôt's castle is attacked by King Meljanz, because Lippaôt's daughter Obîe had rejected the latter's love. For unknown reasons, Obîe tries to discredit Gawain as soon as he arrives at the location. From the top of the castle wall, she and her sister Obilôt watch the stranger and she immediately calls the hero a *koufman* 'trader' (cp. Eschenbach 1961: 352,16), depriving him thus of any knightly attributes. Even though Obîe's mother and sister both object her view, she insists that Gawain is not a knight and continues by saying he would be a *wehselære* 'money lender' (cp. Eschenbach 1961: 353,26). Moreover, she is not satisfied with damaging the protagonist's reputation, she even develops the ambition to get him into trouble. She sends Scherules to Gawain, telling him he were a *koufman* who is trying to trick them. He, however, can judge simply by Gawain's looks that he must be a noble and asks him to be his guest. Obîe is still not giving up and now sends for her father to deal with the *valschære* 'forger' (cp. Eschenbach 1961: 362,24). While she first downgrades his social status as a noble, she now even adds dishonesty to his character. Her father Lippaôt falls for her lies and is quickly on his way, when he meets Scherules whom he tells about the *trügenære* 'defrauder', the *valschære* he was told about. Scherules explains that Lippaôt had been tricked and stresses that the assaulted man is his guest (cp. Eschenbach 1961: 363). In this part of the story, characters exist who defend Gawain against all accusations, like Scherules and Obilôt, who repeatedly calls him a *ritter* 'knight'. Moreover, she is the only character using this term so frequently, probably to compensate for her sister's offending words.

When Gawain meets Orgelûse, however, he is ruthlessly exposed to her insults and humiliations. The protagonist falls in love with her at first sight, but Orgelûse makes clear that she will not accept his love. Nevertheless, he insists on serving her. The woman's way of dealing with such insistent lovers is to permanently insult them and to get them into fights with other knights, hoping that they get killed. After Gawain has completed the first task she has assigned to him, she greets him with "weset willekomen, ir gans" (Eschenbach 1961: 515,13) 'Be welcome, you goose'.

The next noun she uses to insult the hero is *arzet* 'Barber-surgeon' (cp. Eschenbach 1961: 516,30). Gawain had met an injured knight before and now reveals that he knows about the healing abilities of a certain plant, which drives Orgelûse to mock him repeatedly.

When Gawain wants to help the wounded knight, he has to face the fact that he got tricked by the man, as he jumps on the hero's horse and rides off. Gawain being without a horse amuses Orgelûse and she comments the course of events with "vür einen *ritter* ich iuch sach,/dar nâch in kurzen stunden/wurdet ir *arzet* vür die wunden:/nû müezet ir ein *garzûn* wesen." [emphasis mine] (Eschenbach 1961: 523,06) 'First I thought you were a knight. Then, after a few hours, you became a surgeon for wounds and now you seem to be a squire'.

Despite all her efforts, Gawain does not even consider to leave Orgelûse. This is why she eventually mentions that he seems to her to be a 'dumb man' (cp. Eschenbach 1961: 530;10).

Only after Gawain decides to fight against the man who killed Orgelûses husband, and who thus caused her bitterness, the lady suddenly changes, accepts the protagonists love and refers to him as the "ellensrîche" (Eschenbach 1961: 614,11) '(man) rich of courage' and her beloved (cp. Eschenbach 1961: 620,08).

5.4 Expressions Used by the Narrator

Though characters can have their very own view of Gawain as the examples of Orgelûse and Obîe have shown, the narrator can either support their image or intervene. The following part will therefore deal with the analysis of the narrator's expressions.

In *Parzival*, the most frequent expressions the narrator works with to refer to Gawain is *Lôtes sun* or *Lôtes kint* 'Lôt's son/Lôt's child', and is also used exclusively by him (see Figure 4). It can thus be concluded that for the other characters, the relationship between the living relatives is more important and that therefore it is necessary for the narrator to mention the protagonist's descent in order to not lose this information as relationships are a major topic in Eschenbach's work.

Figure 4 – Distribution of Nouns Used by the Narrator in *Parzival*[15]

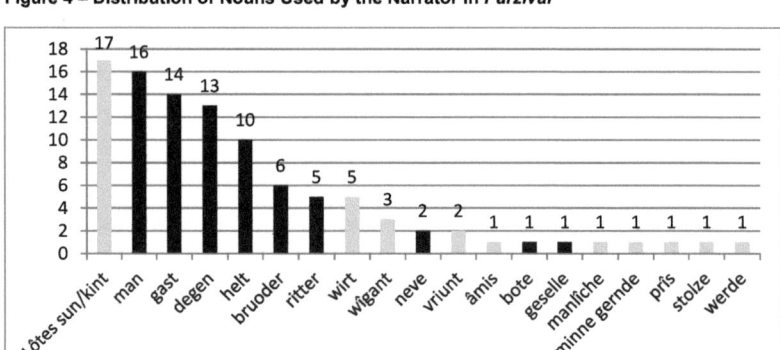

For the commonly used terms, it is difficult to find a distinct semantic feature that is most dominant. While the second most frequent expression is the neutral *man* 'man', *gast* equally conveys 'guest' and 'stranger', whereas *degen* and *helt* imply both [HERO] and [WARRIOR].

Gast with its meaning 'stranger' occurs the last time shortly before Gawain breaks off the twig for Orgelûse (cp. Eschenbach 1961: 601,07). When his love is finally accepted, this seems to be the turning point in the way he is perceived. This accounts also for the term's meaning 'guest': the last time it is mentioned is before the hero sets out to free the ladies at the enchanted castle (cp. Eschenbach 1961: 558,14). After he successfully passes the adventures he encounters on his quest, Gawain becomes lord of Schastel Marveil. He thus has no longer to be a guest at someone else's houses and the noun *wirt* is introduced (cp. Eschenbach 1961: 639,13), denoting the semantic feature [HOST]. This fact, however, is only mentioned by the narrator.

Another aspect exclusively stressed by him both through nouns and adjectives is Gawain's longing for courtly love. It is noteworthy that *minne gernde* only occurs in connection with Orgelûse (cp. Eschenback 1961: 512,19/530,15/615,15). It is not mentioned during the scene in which the protagonist kisses Antikonîe, a kiss which is described as "ungastlîch" (Eschenbach 1961: 405,21) 'intimate'. Shortly after that, Gawain reaches under the lady's coat and touches her hip. It can thus be argued here that this scene deals more with bodily lust while the feeling for Orgelûse is actual love. *Minne gernde* therefore describes the courtly love which is also acceptable in a Christian view and even results in a wedding.

---

[15] Expressions exclusively used by the narrator are marked with gray.

The narrator is also the first to emphasize the extraordinary position Gawain has within the members of the Round Table. He is not just "der werden tavelrunder bote" (Eschenbach 1961: 380,11) 'the messenger of the noble Knights of the Round Table', but even "der tavelrunder hœster prîs" (Eschenbach 1961: 301,07) 'the biggest glory for the Round Table'.

It is especially with regard to adjectives, that the narrator stresses certain already established features, like the hero's bravery, his noble birth and his manliness. Moreover, he enhances the protagonist by further characteristics such as being quick, proud and gracious. In total, the narrator adds 17 completely new adjectives to the list of expressions. The most frequently occurring term, however, is *wert*. It especially emphasizes the features [NOBLE], [COURTLY] and [RESPECTED] and thus focuses on Gawain's social position.[16]

A last aspect is the importance of the narrator in fending off accusations made by minor characters, though this is done by using the predicative adjective *unschuldec* 'innocent' and the noun phrase *âne schulde* 'without guilt'. When Obîe tries to get Gawain in trouble, the narrator is quick to tell the reader that the protagonist receives her hatred without reason (cp. Eschenbach 1961: 360,08) and when her father is on his way to find the *trügenære* his daughter had told him about, the narrator interrupts the dialog between Lippaôt and Scherules with the remark "unschuldec was her Gâwân" (Eschenbach 1961: 363,17) 'Gawain was innocent'.

---

[16] See appendix 'Table 13 - Semantic Features of Adjectives in *Parzival*', page 70.

6. Discussion

After the different findings in regard to the presentation of Gawain in *Parzival* and *Sir Gawain and the Green Knight* have been analyzed, the results will now be summarized and compared in the following.[17] The next chapter will then discuss whether a lexico-semantic approach can offer new aspects of Gawain's character.

6.1 Differences and Similarities in Both Works

In general, the Middle High German Gawain has more different characteristics than the Middle English one. The semantic features [POWERFUL], [POLITE], [CHEERFUL], [WELCOME], [UNWORTHY] and [WEAK] only occur in *Sir Gawain and the Green Knight*. In *Parzival*, apart from terms meant as insults, several expressions can be found which are not conveyed by its English counterpart. Here the protagonist is described as [HERO], [STRANGER], [GUEST], [HOST], [FRIEND], [BELOVED], [MESSENGER] and [TEACHER]. He is not only defined as a nobleman and knight and has a lot more roles to embody. Furthermore, he is ascribed the attributes of being [COURTLY], [GRACIOUS], [GLORIOUS], [PROUD], [QUICK], [UNDISMAYED], [LOVE LONGING] and [RESPECTED] and it is even revealed that he is – different to what one might expect – a Norwegian.

For the Middle English work, the five most frequent semantic features were [NOBLE], [WARRIOR], [BRAVE], [POWERFUL] and [POLITE], whereas the Middle High German text focused on [RELATIVE], [WARRIOR], [NOBLE], [COURTLY] and [RESPECTED]. In addition, the goodness of Gawain was especially stressed in the first work while in the second one, the hero had to face insults and unjustified accusations.

The Middle English Gawain likes to understate himself and refuses to accept the rather heroic image minor characters have of him. As a result, he also has a rather neutral attitude toward his social status. The Middle High German hero represents quite the contrary: he has confidence in himself and his abilities and does not hesitate to express them. The way he sees himself is dependent on the circumstances he faces and he also differentiates between personal and professional matters.

---

[17] For a comparison of all semantic features see 'Figure 5 - Distribution of Semantic Features in Percent' on page 77 in the appendix.

For minor characters in *Sir Gawain and the Green Knight*, the hero has an excellent reputation and represents the ideal knight. This status remains unaffected by any of the protagonist's actions, even when they are contradictory to what is thought of him. Another important feature is Gawain's handsomeness which is frequently expressed by Lord Bertilak's wife. This attribute does not occur in expressions of minor characters in *Parzival*. Here, Gawain is especially perceived as a stranger or guest. Moreover, he is defined by his relationship to his living relatives. Contrary to the Middle English Gawain, the protagonist's impeccable status is repeatedly challenged by minor characters and can only be regained by jousts.

Especially in this regard, the narrator plays an important role in the Middle High German work. He actively defends Gawain against the unjustified accusations and lets the reader know that the hero is innocent. In the Middle English text, the narrator has no need to intervene in such a way as other characters share his opinion of the protagonist and the only one to contradict their views is Gawain himself. Both narrators describe the extraordinary position the hero has within the members of the Round Table and especially stress the semantic features [WARRIOR] and [NOBLE]. A difference can be found for expressions that depend on certain events. In *Sir Gawain and the Green Knight*, all terms were used throughout the work but in *Parzival*, the nouns *guest* and *stranger* disappeared when Gawain became lord of his own castle and was thus referred to as *host*.

6.2 Discussion of the Advantages of a Lexico-Semantic Analysis

As the differences and similarities of both works have now been analyzed, the following abstract will deal with the question whether a lexico-semantic approach offers further insights into the characterization of Gawain.

To start with, the Middle English hero's qualities will be discussed. The extraordinary status Gawain achieved within the Knights of the Round Table and the high opinion the narrator and Lord Bertilak have of the protagonist can also be found in Davenport's article (cp. 2006: 274) and do thus not necessarily derive from a focus on semantic aspects. This accounts for the protagonist's attractiveness (Thompson/Busby 2006: 1) and politeness (Davenport 2006: 284) as well.

The only mentioning of Gawain's tendency to downgrade himself is partly captured in what Davenport calls "a sympathetic lack of aggressive self-confidence" (2006: 277). The question arises what *aggressive* exactly means in this context. On the one hand, it can be agreed that the hero does not talk proudly about his belief in himself and his abilities in public. On the other hand, this would mean that Gawain nevertheless has self-confidence but which he does not express verbally. In that case, only two instances occur in which he has the possibility to indirectly demonstrate that he believes in his abilities. The first occasion is when he offers to strike the blow against the Green Knight instead of Arthur, but taking part in this Christmas game is not so much a question of self-confidence – every slightly skilled knight at the Round Table would be able to cut off another one's head when he does not have to expect any resistance from his opponent – but rather a question of courage to face whatever consequences this game brings. Moreover, any self-confidence in that scene would be totally replaced by his extreme self-debasement.

The fact that Gawain keeps his promise to meet the Green Knight could be regarded as the second occasion in which he is able to demonstrate confidence in himself. However, it becomes even more apparent in that section that his action is more about feeling obliged to his word than trusting in his abilities. Otherwise, he would not have kept the girdle in order to protect himself and the protagonist is well aware that unlike the Green Knight, he is not able to restore his head (cp. *SGGK*, 63). Concluding from these observations, Davenport does not sufficiently grasp Gawain's character here and the semantic approach helps to detect the more subtle differences between self-confidence, courage and the feeling of obligation to stay true to one's word.

An aspect which did not occur in the semantic approach is the hero's fear. Regarding the collected nouns and adjectives, evidence for the protagonist being a careful man who tries to avoid dangers or mistakes and rather takes no risks could not be found. However, this fact is mentioned by Davenport (cp. 2006: 277) and is visible for example in the scene where the Green Knight pretends the first time to hit the protagonist: when Gawain sees the blade rushing down on him, he winces (*SGGK*, 62). Davenport argues that the mistake the protagonist made was not feeling fear but giving in to it and following natural instincts rather than sticking to courtly ideals (2006: 285). Here, the importance of taking verbs into account becomes obvious as otherwise, this aspect would be missing. Nevertheless, the semantic analysis of this book offers another perspective on Gawain's fear. As the idea of the hero being afraid is not expressed by an attributive adjective as in *the fearful man* or by a nominalized adjective, this idea is not of such significance as for example the hero's courtliness. It is not denied that there are situations in which Gawain feels fear, but it is also not a characteristic that defines him. Here, the semantic analysis helps to differentiate between different levels of significance in regard to the features the expressions convey.

However, from Davenport's point of view, this unknightly behavior means that Gawain's role as a hero is uncertain and "the ending of the poem is designed to make us wonder whether Gawain has fulfilled such a role or not" (2006: 274).

For the Middle High German hero, the same weakness can be found. When the protagonist has to face the angry mob after he kissed Antikonîe, the narrator tells the reader that Gawain "was [...] grôz angest kunt" (Eschenbach 1961: 417,10) 'felt great fear'. Moreover, he can also be found crying and he faints two times after a strenuous fight (Homberger 1970: 127). In contrast to Davenport, neither Homberger nor Classen doubt that Gawain is nevertheless a hero and again, those frailties are not expressed by attributive adjectives or nouns.

Further facets of Gawain's character are his strong believe in God (cp. Classen 2006: 219) and his tendency to reflect about a situation rather than engaging into a fierce battle. When Parzival, who is not yet a member of the Knights of the Round Table, is discovered close to Arthur's camp, staring onto three blood drops on the ground, Segramors and Keie interpret his silence as a demand for a fight, but both lose the joust. Gawain, on the other hand,

> does not even equip himself with weapons or armor when he leaves camp to discover the identity of the stranger. At first he cannot understand why Parzival fails to respond to his entreaties to accompany him to see King Arthur. Guided by wisdom and courtly manners, however, he recognizes that Parzival is under a love spell.
>
> (Classen 2006: 218)

At another occasion (cp. Eschenbach 1961: 538), Gawain is not able to avoid a fight and after he has won the joust and brought his opponent to the ground, he asks the other knight to guarantee him safety in order to let him live. Although the latter denies him this wish and claims he would rather die, the protagonist refuses to kill the man. This is followed by a second attack on Gawain and once again, he is able to fend off his enemy. Instead of changing his mind, the hero repeats his wish for safety but his opponent still rejects his request. Gawain recognizes, however, that the other knight acts out of love for Orgelûse – like he does as well – and he decides that despite what has happened he cannot kill his opponent for both did not fight out of free will, but were forced to do so by love.

7. Conclusion

Though Eschenbach as well as the *Gawain*-Poet rely on Chrétien de Troyes' *Conte du Graal*, only the basic features can be found for both protagonists. The more detail is added to the figures, the more they differ in their characteristics. The biggest contrast is in their self-perception, whereas narrators and minor characters in both works agree on the excellent image they have of Gawain and constantly keep a high opinion of him. Apart from his outstanding reputation, narrator and minor characters of *Sir Gawain and the Green Knight* focus on nobility and fighting skills, whereas in *Parzival*, kinship is of greater importance.

Contrary to the Middle English text, a lexico-semantic analysis of nouns and attributive adjectives for the Middle High German Gawain did not bring further insights for the protagonist's characterization. Nevertheless, it became clear that this approach opens up the possibility to detect subtle differences in the emphasis of certain characteristics. In order to achieve a thorough result, it is necessary to enhance the study by verbs, adverbs, predicative adjectives and those nouns which are used to describe Gawain's manner. Aspects like the Middle English Gawain's arrogant pride (SGGK, 19) or the Middle High German hero's frequent sorrow (Eschenbach 1961: 513,09) did not occur in the analysis of this book but convey important aspects that have to be considered in order to gain two fully comparable figures.

Further research could also be done in regard to how Gawain is depicted in today's adaptions of the Knights of the Round Table (e.g. films) compared to the image that was conveyed in the Middle Ages. Has his character still so many facets or does the perception of what an admirable protagonist is nowadays not allow him to show for example fear anymore? Analyzing the way he and minor characters refer to him might not only show differences in his perception but might also illustrate whether there are changes in the characteristics we value in order to think of someone as a hero. Linking the old with the new could thus possibly give us a better understanding of our today's society.

Primary Sources

Eschenbach, Wolfram (von). 1961. *Parzival*. Ed. Albert Leitzmann. Tübingen: Niemeyer. Access: Thesaurus Indogermanischer Text- und Sprachmaterialien (TITUS). Besides printed version also URL: http://titus.fkidg1.uni-frankfurt.de/texte/etcs/germ/mhd/parzival/parzi.htm? parzi001.htm# Wolfram_Parzival_1 (last accessed August 29, 2014).

Sir Gawain and the Green Knight. Ed. J.R.R. Tolkien & E. V. Gordon. Oxford: Clarendon Press. 1967. Also accessed via: Corpus of Middle English Prose and Verse. URL: http://quod.lib.umich.edu/c/cme/Gawain? rgn=main;view=fulltext;q1=Gawain (last accessed August 29, 2014).

Secondary Sources

Barron, William R.J. 1994. *Sir Gawain and the Green Knight*. Manchester: Manchester UP.

Bennet, Michael J. 1997. "The Historical Background". In: Brewer, Derek & Jonathan Gibson (eds.). *A Companion to the* Gawain-*Poet*. Cambridge: Brewer. 71-90.

Borroff, Marie. 1996. "Systematic Sound Symbolism in the Long Alliterative Line in 'Beowulf' and 'Sir Gawain'". In: C.B. McCully & J.J. Anderson (eds.). *English Historical Metrics*. Cambridge: Cambridge UP. 120-133.

Brewer, Derek. 1997. "Introduction" In: Brewer, Derek & Jonathan Gibson (eds.). *A Companion to the* Gawain-*Poet*. Cambridge: Brewer. 1-21.

Brewer, Elizabeth. 1997. "The Sources of *Sir Gawain and the Green Knight*" In: Brewer, Derek & Jonathan Gibson (eds.). *A Companion to the* Gawain-*Poet*. Cambridge: Brewer. 243-256.

Bumke, Joachim. 1970. *Wolfram von Eschenbach*. Stuttgart: Metzler.

Classen, Albrecht. 2006. "Crisis and Triumph in the World of Medieval Knighthood and Chivalry: Gawan in Wolfram von Eschenbach's *Parzival*". In: Thompson, Raymond H. & Keith Busby (eds.). *Gawain: A Casebook*. New York: Routledge.217-219.

Davenport, William A. 2006. "*Sir Gawain and the Green Knight*: The Poet's Treatment of the Hero and His Adventure". In: Thompson, Thompson, Raymond H. & Keith Busby (eds.). *Gawain: A Casebook*. New York: Routledge. 273-286.

Homberger, Dietrich. 1970. *Gawein: Untersuchung zur mittelhochdeutschen Artusepik*. Bochum.

OAAD. "Apposition" in *Oxford Advanced American Dictionary*. Oxford UP. URL: http://oaadonline.oxfordlearnersdictionaries.com/dictionary/apposition (last accessed October 4, 2014).

Thompson, Raymond H. & Keith Busby (eds.). 2006. *Gawain: A Casebook*. New York: Routledge.

Turville-Petre, Thorlac. 1977. *The Alliterative Revival*. Cambridge: Brewer.

URL 1: http://quod.lib.umich.edu/cgi/m/mec/med-idx?type=id&id=MED24418 (last accessed August 29, 2014).

URL 2: http://quod.lib.umich.edu/cgi/m/mec/med-idx?type=id&id=MED52699 (last accessed August 29, 2014).

URL 3: http://quod.lib.umich.edu/cgi/m/mec/med-idx?type=id&id=MED26710 (last accessed August 29, 2014).

URL 4: http://quod.lib.umich.edu/cgi/m/mec/med-idx?type=id&id=MED4195 (last accessed August 29, 2014).

URL 5: http://quod.lib.umich.edu/cgi/m/mec/med-idx?type=id&id=MED24956 (last accessed August 29, 2014).

URL   6:   http://quod.lib.umich.edu/cgi/m/mec/med-idx?type=id&id=MED39202 (last accessed August 29, 2014).

URL   7:   http://quod.lib.umich.edu/cgi/m/mec/med-idx?type=id&id=MED17625 (last accessed August 29, 2014).

URL   8:   http://quod.lib.umich.edu/cgi/m/mec/med-idx?type=id&id=MED20105 (last accessed August 29, 2014).

URL   9:   http://quod.lib.umich.edu/cgi/m/mec/med-idx?type=id&id=MED34652 (last accessed August 29, 2014).

URL   10:   http://quod.lib.umich.edu/cgi/m/mec/med-idx?type=id&id=MED36795 (last accessed August 29, 2014).

URL   11:   http://quod.lib.umich.edu/cgi/m/mec/med-idx?type=id&id=MED20378 (last accessed August 29, 2014).

URL   12:   http://quod.lib.umich.edu/cgi/m/mec/med-idx?type=id&id=MED11195 (last accessed August 29, 2014).

URL   13:   http://quod.lib.umich.edu/cgi/m/mec/med-idx?type=id&id=MED8546 (last accessed August 29, 2014).

URL   14:   http://www.oxforddictionaries.com/definition/english/cousin   (last accessed August 29, 2014).

URL   15:   http://quod.lib.umich.edu/cgi/m/mec/med-idx?type=id&id=MED19067 (last accessed August 29, 2014).

URL   16:   http://quod.lib.umich.edu/cgi/m/mec/med-idx?type=id&id=MED18403 (last accessed August 29, 2014).

URL   17:   http://quod.lib.umich.edu/cgi/m/mec/med-idx?type=id&id=MED29608 (last accessed August 29, 2014).

URL 18: http://quod.lib.umich.edu/cgi/m/mec/med-idx?type=id&id=MED38720 (last accessed August 29, 2014).

URL 19: http://quod.lib.umich.edu/cgi/m/mec/med-idx?type=id&id=MED42606 (last accessed August 29, 2014).

URL 20: http://quod.lib.umich.edu/cgi/m/mec/med-idx?type=id&id=MED47337 (last accessed August 29, 2014).

URL 21: http://quod.lib.umich.edu/cgi/m/mec/med-idx?type=id&id=MED53242 (last accessed August 29, 2014).

URL 22: http://quod.lib.umich.edu/cgi/m/mec/med-idx?type=id&id=MED53317 (last accessed August 29, 2014).

URL 23: http://quod.lib.umich.edu/cgi/m/mec/med-idx?type=id&id=MED18947 (last accessed August 29, 2014).

URL 24: http://quod.lib.umich.edu/cgi/m/mec/med-idx?type=id&id=MED5427 (last accessed August 29, 2014).

URL 25: http://quod.lib.umich.edu/cgi/m/mec/med-idx?type=id&id=MED17599 (last accessed August 29, 2014).

URL 26: http://quod.lib.umich.edu/cgi/m/mec/med-idx?type=id&id=MED26256 (last accessed August 29, 2014).

URL 27: http://quod.lib.umich.edu/cgi/m/mec/med-idx?type=id&id=MED42913 (last accessed August 29, 2014).

URL 28: http://quod.lib.umich.edu/cgi/m/mec/med-idx?type=id&id=MED11216 (last accessed August 29, 2014).

URL 29: http://quod.lib.umich.edu/cgi/m/mec/med-idx?type=id&id=MED15377 (last accessed August 29, 2014).

URL 30: http://quod.lib.umich.edu/cgi/m/mec/med-idx?type=id&id=MED18063
(last accessed August 29, 2014).

URL 31: http://quod.lib.umich.edu/cgi/m/mec/med-idx?type=id&id=MED27890
(last accessed August 29, 2014).

URL 32: http://quod.lib.umich.edu/cgi/m/mec/med-idx?type=id&id=MED29610
(last accessed August 29, 2014).

URL 33: http://quod.lib.umich.edu/cgi/m/mec/med-idx?type=id&id=MED40301
(last accessed August 29, 2014).

URL 34: http://quod.lib.umich.edu/cgi/m/mec/med-idx?type=id&id=MED46999
(last accessed August 29, 2014).

URL 35: http://quod.lib.umich.edu/cgi/m/mec/med-idx?type=id&id=MED52084
(last accessed August 29, 2014).

URL 36: http://quod.lib.umich.edu/cgi/m/mec/med-idx?type=id&id=MED50284
(last accessed August 29, 2014).

URL 37: http://quod.lib.umich.edu/cgi/m/mec/med-idx?type=id&id=MED5205
(last accessed August 29, 2014).

URL 38: http://woerterbuchnetz.de/cgi-bin/WBNetz/wbgui_py?sigle=Lexer&
mode=Vernetzung&hitlist=&patternlist=&lemid=LM00250 (last accessed
August 29, 2014).

URL 39: http://woerterbuchnetz.de/cgi-bin/WBNetz/wbgui_py?sigle=Lexer&
mode=Vernetzung&hitlist=&patternlist=&lemid=LG00337 (last accessed
August 29, 2014).

URL 40: http://woerterbuchnetz.de/cgi-bin/WBNetz/wbgui_py?sigle=Lexer&
mode=Vernetzung&hitlist=&patternlist=&lemid=LS09003 (last accessed
August 29, 2014).

URL 41: http://woerterbuchnetz.de/cgi-bin/WBNetz/wbgui_py?sigle=Lexer& mode=Vernetzung&hitlist=&patternlist=&lemid=LK01268 (last accessed August 29, 2014).

URL 42: http://woerterbuchnetz.de/cgi-bin/WBNetz/wbgui_py?sigle=Lexer& mode=Vernetzung&hitlist=&patternlist=&lemid=LN00808 (last accessed August 29, 2014).

URL 43: http://woerterbuchnetz.de/cgi-bin/WBNetz/wbgui_py?sigle=Lexer& mode=Vernetzung&lemid=LR01453 (last accessed August 29, 2014).

URL 44: http://woerterbuchnetz.de/cgi-bin/WBNetz/wbgui_py?sigle=Lexer& mode=Vernetzung&hitlist=&patternlist=&lemid=LH01577 (last accessed August 29, 2014).

URL 45: http://woerterbuchnetz.de/cgi-bin/WBNetz/wbgui_py?sigle=Lexer& mode=Vernetzung&hitlist=&patternlist=&lemid=LD00168 (last accessed August 29, 2014).

URL 46: http://woerterbuchnetz.de/cgi-bin/WBNetz/wbgui_py?sigle=Lexer& mode=Vernetzung&hitlist=&patternlist=&lemid=LB04192 (last accessed August 29, 2014).

URL 47: http://woerterbuchnetz.de/cgi-bin/WBNetz/wbgui_py?sigle=Lexer& mode=Vernetzung&hitlist=&patternlist=&lemid=LW03799 (last accessed August 29, 2014).

URL 48: http://woerterbuchnetz.de/cgi-bin/WBNetz/wbgui_py?sigle=Lexer& mode=Vernetzung&hitlist=&patternlist=&lemid=LW03024 (last accessed August 29, 2014).

URL 49: http://woerterbuchnetz.de/cgi-bin/WBNetz/wbgui_py?sigle=Lexer& mode=Vernetzung&hitlist=&patternlist=&lemid=LV06059 (last accessed August 29, 2014).

URL 50: http://woerterbuchnetz.de/cgi-bin/WBNetz/wbgui_py?sigle=Lexer&
mode=Vernetzung&hitlist=&patternlist=&lemid=LB03546 (last accessed
August 29, 2014).

URL 51: http://woerterbuchnetz.de/cgi-bin/WBNetz/wbgui_py?sigle=Lexer&
mode=Vernetzung&hitlist=&patternlist=&lemid=LA01202 (last accessed
August 29, 2014).

URL 52: http://woerterbuchnetz.de/cgi-bin/WBNetz/wbgui_py?sigle=Lexer&
mode=Vernetzung&lemid=LS07841 (last accessed August 29, 2014).

URL 53: http://woerterbuchnetz.de/cgi-bin/WBNetz/wbgui_py?sigle=Lexer&
mode=Vernetzung&hitlist=&patternlist=&lemid=LW01938 (last accessed
August 29, 2014).

URL 54: http://woerterbuchnetz.de/cgi-bin/WBNetz/wbgui_py?sigle=Lexer&
mode=Vernetzung&hitlist=&patternlist=&lemid=LG02512 (last accessed
August 29, 2014).

URL 55: http://woerterbuchnetz.de/cgi-bin/WBNetz/wbgui_py?sigle=Lexer&
mode=Vernetzung&hitlist=&patternlist=&lemid=LM00388 (last accessed
August 29, 2014).

URL 56: http://woerterbuchnetz.de/cgi-bin/WBNetz/wbgui_py?sigle=Lexer&
mode=Vernetzung&hitlist=&patternlist=&lemid=LE00701 (last accessed
August 29, 2014).

URL 57: http://woerterbuchnetz.de/cgi-bin/WBNetz/wbgui_py?sigle=Lexer&
mode=Vernetzung&hitlist=&patternlist=&lemid=LE01921 (last accessed
August 29, 2014).

URL 58: http://woerterbuchnetz.de/cgi-bin/WBNetz/wbgui_py?sigle=Lexer&
mode=Vernetzung&hitlist=&patternlist=&lemid=LL00415 (last accessed
August 29, 2014).

URL 59: http://woerterbuchnetz.de/cgi-bin/WBNetz/wbgui_py?sigle=Lexer&
mode=Vernetzung&hitlist=&patternlist=&lemid=LP01421 (last accessed
August 29, 2014).

URL 60: http://woerterbuchnetz.de/cgi-bin/WBNetz/wbgui_py?sigle=Lexer&
mode=Vernetzung&hitlist=&patternlist=&lemid=LM01056 (last accessed
August 29, 2014).

URL 61: http://woerterbuchnetz.de/cgi-bin/WBNetz/wbgui_py?sigle=Lexer&
mode=Vernetzung&lemid=LD00170 (last accessed August 29, 2014).

URL 62: http://woerterbuchnetz.de/cgi-bin/WBNetz/wbgui_py?sigle=Lexer&
mode=Vernetzung&hitlist=&patternlist=&lemid=LS09883 (last accessed
August 29, 2014).

URL 63: http://woerterbuchnetz.de/cgi-bin/WBNetz/wbgui_py?sigle=Lexer&
mode=Vernetzung&hitlist=&patternlist=&lemid=LG02918 (last accessed
August 29, 2014).

URL 64: http://woerterbuchnetz.de/cgi-bin/WBNetz/wbgui_py?sigle=Lexer&
mode=Vernetzung&hitlist=&patternlist=&lemid=LA02123 (last accessed
August 29, 2014).

URL 65: http://woerterbuchnetz.de/cgi-bin/WBNetz/wbgui_py?sigle=Lexer&
mode=Vernetzung&lemid=LK02876 (last accessed August 29, 2014).

URL 66: http://woerterbuchnetz.de/cgi-bin/WBNetz/wbgui_py?sigle=Lexer&
mode=Vernetzung&hitlist=&patternlist=&lemid=LG00335 (last accessed
August 29, 2014).

URL 67: http://woerterbuchnetz.de/cgi-bin/WBNetz/wbgui_py?sigle=Lexer&
mode=Vernetzung&hitlist=&patternlist=&lemid=LT02068 (last accessed
August 29, 2014).

URL   68:   http://woerterbuchnetz.de/cgi-bin/WBNetz/wbgui_py?sigle=Lexer&
mode=Vernetzung&hitlist=&patternlist=&lemid=LV00137 (last accessed
August 29, 2014).

URL   69:   http://woerterbuchnetz.de/cgi-bin/WBNetz/wbgui_py?sigle=Lexer&
mode=Vernetzung&hitlist=&patternlist=&lemid=LW01286 (last accessed
August 29, 2014).

URL   70:   http://woerterbuchnetz.de/cgi-bin/WBNetz/wbgui_py?sigle=Lexer&
mode=Vernetzung&hitlist=&patternlist=&lemid=LT02441 (last accessed
August 29, 2014).

URL   71:   http://woerterbuchnetz.de/cgi-bin/WBNetz/wbgui_py?sigle=Lexer&
mode=Vernetzung&hitlist=&patternlist=&lemid=LM01056 (last accessed
August 29, 2014).

URL   72:   http://woerterbuchnetz.de/cgi-bin/WBNetz/wbgui_py?sigle=Lexer&
mode=Vernetzung&hitlist=&patternlist=&lemid=LK04187 (last accessed
August 29, 2014).

URL   73:   http://woerterbuchnetz.de/cgi-bin/WBNetz/wbgui_py?sigle=Lexer&
mode=Vernetzung&hitlist=&patternlist=&lemid=LS00194 (last accessed
August 29, 2014).

URL   74:   http://woerterbuchnetz.de/cgi-bin/WBNetz/wbgui_py?sigle=Lexer&
mode=Vernetzung&hitlist= &patternlist=&lemid=LG01986 (last accessed
August 29, 2014).

URL   75:   http://woerterbuchnetz.de/cgi-bin/WBNetz/wbgui_py?sigle=Lexer&
mode=Vernetzung&lemid=LB00177 (last accessed August 29, 2014).

URL   76:   http://woerterbuchnetz.de/cgi-bin/WBNetz/wbgui_py?sigle=Lexer&
mode=Vernetzung&hitlist=&patternlist=&lemid=LB01405 (last accessed
August 29, 2014).

URL 77: http://woerterbuchnetz.de/cgi-bin/WBNetz/wbgui_py?sigle=Lexer& mode=Vernetzung&lemid=LH03562 (last accessed August 29, 2014).

URL 78: http://woerterbuchnetz.de/cgi-bin/WBNetz/wbgui_py?sigle=Lexer& mode=Vernetzung&lemid=LV05789 (last accessed August 29, 2014).

URL 79: http://woerterbuchnetz.de/cgi-bin/WBNetz/wbgui_py?sigle=BMZ& mode=Vernetzung&lemid=BS04430 (last accessed August 29, 2014)

URL 80: http://woerterbuchnetz.de/cgi-bin/WBNetz/wbgui_py?mode= Vernetzung&hitlist=&patternlist=&lemid=BZ00044&sigle=BMZ (last accessed August 29, 2014).

URL 81: http://woerterbuchnetz.de/cgi-bin/WBNetz/wbgui_py?sigle=Lexer& mode=Vernetzung&hitlist=&patternlist=&lemid=LW01847 (last accessed August 29, 2014)

URL 82: http://woerterbuchnetz.de/cgi-bin/WBNetz/wbgui_py?mode= Vernetzung&hitlist=&patternlist=&lemid=LG03566&sigle=Lexer (last accessed August 29, 2014).

URL 83: http://woerterbuchnetz.de/cgi-bin/WBNetz/wbgui_py?sigle=Lexer& mode=Vernetzung&lemid=LA00716 (last accessed August 29, 2014).

URL 84: http://woerterbuchnetz.de/cgi-bin/WBNetz/wbgui_py?sigle=Lexer& mode=Vernetzung&lemid=LE00186 (last accessed August 29, 2014).

URL 85: http://woerterbuchnetz.de/cgi-bin/WBNetz/wbgui_py?sigle=Lexer& mode=Vernetzung&lemid=LE00719 (last accessed August 29, 2014).

URL 86: http://woerterbuchnetz.de/cgi-bin/WBNetz/wbgui_py?sigle=Lexer& mode=Vernetzung&hitlist=&patternlist=&lemid=LK00220 (last accessed August 29, 2014).

URL 87: http://woerterbuchnetz.de/cgi-bin/WBNetz/wbgui_py?sigle=Lexer& mode=Vernetzung&lemid=LM01819 (last accessed August 29, 2014).

URL 88: http://woerterbuchnetz.de/cgi-bin/WBNetz/wbgui_py?sigle=Lexer&
mode=Vernetzung&lemid=LS06975 (last accessed August 29, 2014).

URL 89: http://woerterbuchnetz.de/cgi-bin/WBNetz/wbgui_py?sigle=Lexer&
mode=Vernetzung&lemid=LT02463 (last accessed August 29, 2014).

URL 90: http://woerterbuchnetz.de/cgi-bin/WBNetz/wbgui_py?sigle=Lexer&
mode=Vernetzung&lemid=LL01467 (last accessed August 29, 2014).

URL 91: http://woerterbuchnetz.de/cgi-bin/WBNetz/wbgui_py?sigle=FindeB&
mode=Vernetzung&hitlist=&patternlist=&lemid=FG02688 (last accessed
August 29, 2014).

URL 92: http://woerterbuchnetz.de/cgi-bin/WBNetz/wbgui_py?sigle=Lexer&
mode=Vernetzung&lemid=LS08793 (last accessed August 29, 2014).

URL 93: http://woerterbuchnetz.de/cgi-bin/WBNetz/wbgui_py?sigle=Lexer&
mode=Vernetzung&lemid=LG03684 (last accessed August 29, 2014).

URL 94: http://woerterbuchnetz.de/cgi-bin/WBNetz/wbgui_py?sigle=Lexer&
mode=Vernetzung&lemid=LG06127 (last accessed August 29, 2014).

URL 95: http://woerterbuchnetz.de/Lexer/?sigle=Lexer&mode=Vernetzung&
lemid=LB04209 (last accessed August 29, 2014).

Index of Figures

Figure 1 - Most Frequent Nouns for *Sir Gawain and the Green Knight* 17

Figure 2 – Distribution of Nouns Used by the Narrator in *Sir Gawain and the Green Knight*..22

Figure 3 - Most Frequent Nouns for *Parzival* 25

Figure 4 – Distribution of Nouns Used by the Narrator in *Parzival*....................32

Figure 5 - Distribution of Semantic Features in Percent 81

Index of Tables

Table 1 - Distribution of Semantic Features in *SGGK*...18

Table 2 - Distribution of Semantic Features in *Parzival* 27

Table 3 - Collection of Nouns for *Sir Gawain and the Green Knight*..................52

Table 4 - Collection of Adjectives for *Sir Gawain and the Green Knight*............56

Table 5 - Collection of Appositions for *Sir Gawain and the Green Knight*..........56

Table 6 - Semantic Features of Nouns in *Sir Gawain and the Green Knight*.....57

Table 7 - Semantic Features of Adjectives in *Sir Gawain and the Green Knight*..59

Table 8 - Semantic Features of Appositions in *Sir Gawain and the Green Knight*..60

Table 9 - Collection of Nouns for *Parzival*...61

Table 10 - Collection of Adjectives for *Parzival*...65

Table 11 - Collection of Appositions for *Parzival*...66

Table 12 - Semantic Features of Nouns in *Parzival*..67

Table 13 - Semantic Features of Adjectives in *Parzival*......................................74

Table 14 - Semantic Features of Appositions in *Parzival*....................................79

Appendices

I. Complete Data for *Sir Gawain and the Green Knight*

Table 3 - Collection of Nouns for *Sir Gawain and the Green Knight*

	Noun	Verse Line	User
1	burne	776	N
2	burne	779	N
3	burne	785	N
4	burne	1631	N
5	burne	1779	N
6	burne	1834	N
7	burne	925	O (Green Knight)
8	burne	1071	O (Green Knight)
9	burne	2338	O (Green Knight)
10	burne	1189	N
11	burne	2024	N
12	burne	2071	N
13	burne	2315	N
14	burne	2320	N
15	burnes	481	N
16	buurne	825	N
17	comly	674	O
18	cosyn	372	O (Arthur)
19	dere	928	N
20	dere	1798	O (Lady)
21	feblest	354	G
22	frek	651	N
23	freke	641	N
24	freke	803	N
25	freke	894	N
26	freke	1282	N
27	freke	1294	N
28	freke	1315	N
29	freke	1925	N
30	freke	2373	N
31	freke	2274	O (Green Knight)
32	freke	2363	O (Green Knight)
33	frekez	537	N
34	gome	748	N
35	haþel	655	N
36	haþel	771	N
37	haþel	1641	N
38	haþel	379	O (Green Knight)
39	haþel	2467	O (Green Knight)
40	haþel	2065	N
41	hende	827	N
42	hende	1252	O (Lady)

43	hende	1813	O (Lady)
44	ientyle	542	N
45	kniʒtes	111	N
46	knyʒt	1279	G
47	knyʒt	1538	G
48	knyʒt	366	N
49	knyʒt	381	N
50	knyʒt	482	N
51	knyʒt	557	N
52	knyʒt	562	N
53	knyʒt	631	N
54	knyʒt	639	N
55	knyʒt	648	N
56	knyʒt	656	N
57	knyʒt	709	N
58	knyʒt	734	N
59	knyʒt	736	N
60	knyʒt	810	N
61	knyʒt	816	N
62	knyʒt	869	N
63	knyʒt	941	N
64	knyʒt	1043	N
65	knyʒt	1088	N
66	knyʒt	1261	N
67	knyʒt	1476	N
68	knyʒt	1629	N
69	knyʒt	1657	N
70	knyʒt	1670	N
71	knyʒt	1731	N
72	knyʒt	1769	N
73	knyʒt	1788	N
74	knyʒt	1855	N
75	knyʒt	1869	N
76	knyʒt	1978	N
77	knyʒt	2034	N
78	knyʒt	2154	N
79	knyʒt	2175	N
80	knyʒt	2185	N
81	knyʒt	2212	N
82	knyʒt	2489	N
83	knyʒt	2492	N
84	knyʒt	2513	N
85	knyʒt	2273	O (Green Knight)
86	knyʒt	1225	O (Lady)
87	knyʒt	1272	O (Lady)
88	knyʒt	1520	O (Lady)
89	lede	540	N
90	lede	1195	N

91	lede	1469	N
92	lede	1560	N
93	lede	2095	O (servant)
94	leude	675	N
95	leude	908	N
96	leude	1306	N
97	leude	2505	N
98	leude	1109	O (Green Knight)
99	Leude	1675	O (Green Knight)
100	leude	2006	N
101	leude	2333	N
102	lude	449	O (Green Knight)
103	mon	1538	G
104	mon	570	N
105	mon	644	N
106	mon	718	N
107	mon	834	N
108	mon	878	N
109	mon	898	N
110	mon	1179	N
111	mon	1263	N
112	mon	1492	N
113	mon	1633	N
114	mon	1871	N
115	mon	1961	N
116	mon	2043	N
117	mon	2290	N
118	mon	2369	N
119	mon	2350	O (Green Knight)
120	mon	1746	O (Lady)
121	mon	1800	O (Lady)
122	noble	1750	N
123	prynce	623	N
124	prynce	830	N
125	prynce	873	N
126	prynce	902	N
127	prynce	2072	N
128	prynce	2269	N
129	renk	691	N
130	renk	1558	N
131	renk	1821	N
132	renk	2337	N
133	schalk	1776	N
134	segge	763	N
135	segge	848	N
136	segge	893	N
137	segge	1050	N
138	segge	1091	N

139	segge	1385	N
140	segge	1637	N
141	segge	394	O (Green Knight)
142	segge	574	N
143	segge	622	N
144	segge	1658	N
145	segge	2407	N
146	segge	2518	N
147	sistersunes	111	N
148	stalworth	1659	N
149	tulk	638	N
150	wakkest	354	G
151	wlonk	1989	N
152	wyȝ	819	N
153	wyȝ	581	N
154	wyȝe	1039	G
155	wyȝe	1244	G
156	wyȝe	715	N
157	wyȝe	887	N
158	wyȝe	945	N
159	wyȝe	1276	N
160	wyȝe	1381	N
161	wyȝe	1660	N
162	wyȝe	1801	N
163	wyȝe	938	N
164	wyȝe	814	O
165	wyȝe	1482	O (Lady)
166	wyȝe	1508	O (Lady)
167	wyȝe	1743	N
168	wyȝe	2037	N
169	wyȝe	2050	N
170	wyȝe	2240	O (Green Knight)
171	wyȝe	2469	O (Green Knight)
172	wyȝe	2091	O (servant)
173	wyghe	1487	N

Table 4 - Collection of Adjectives for *Sir Gawain and the Green Knight*

	Adjective	Verse Line	User
1	bolde	1631	N
2	bolde	2043	N
3	bolde	2338	O (Green Knight)
4	comloker	869	N
5	comlokest	1520	O (Lady)
6	comlyche	648	N
7	derf	1492	N
8	fautlest	2363	O (Green Knight)
9	fre	803	N
10	fre	1961	N
11	gay	666	N
12	gentyle	2185	N
13	gentylest	639	N
14	god	1179	N
15	gode	2214	G
16	gode	109	N
17	gode	2491	N
18	gode	482	N
19	goode	381	N
20	goude	2118	O (servant)
21	hende	1731	N
22	hende	1633	N
23	luflych	1657	N
24	luflych	1469	N
25	myry	1263	N
26	noble	623	N
27	siker	111,00	N
28	stif	570	N
29	stif	2369	N
30	trwe	1091	N
31	vnworþy	1244	G
32	welcomest	938	N

Table 5 - Collection of Appositions for *Sir Gawain and the Green Knight*

	Phrase	Verse Line	User
1	Gawan þe hende	405	N
2	Gawayn þe blyþe	1213	N
3	Gawayn þe gode	1110	N
4	Gawayn þe noble	2149	N
5	Sir Gawayn þe gode	1926	N

II. Semantic Features in *Sir Gawain and the Green Knight*

Table 6 - Semantic Features of Nouns in *Sir Gawain and the Green Knight*

	knyȝt (URL 1)	wyȝe (URL 2)	mon (URL 3)	burne (URL 4)	le(u)de (URL 5)	segge (URL 6)
[NOBLE]	+	-	-	+	-	-
[WARRIOR]	+	-	-	+	-	-
[BRAVE]	-	-	-	-	-	-
[POWERFUL]	-	-	-	-	-	-
[HANDSOME]	-	-	-	-	-	-
[POLITE]	-	-	-	-	-	-
[GOOD]	-	-	-	-	-	-
[STRONG]	-	-	-	-	-	-
[CHEERFUL]	-	-	-	-	-	-
[KIND]	-	-	-	-	-	-
[RELATIVE]	-	-	-	-	-	-
[DEAR]	-	-	-	-	-	-
[WEAK]	-	-	-	-	-	-
[LOYAL]	-	-	-	-	-	-
[WELCOME]	-	-	-	-	-	-
[UNWORTHY]	-	-	-	-	-	-
[FAULTLESS]	-	-	-	-	-	-

	freke (URL 7)	haþel (URL 8)	prynce (URL 9)	renk[18] (URL 10)	hende (URL 11)	dere (URL 12)
[NOBLE]	-	+	+	-	+	+
[WARRIOR]	+	+	+	+	-	-
[BRAVE]	+	-	-	-	+	+
[POWERFUL]	-	-	-	-	+	-
[POLITE]	-	-	-	-	+	-
[GOOD]	-	-	-	-	-	-
[HANDSOME]	-	-	-	-	-	-
[STRONG]	-	-	-	-	-	-
[CHEERFUL]	-	-	-	-	-	-
[KIND]	-	-	-	-	-	-
[RELATIVE]	-	-	-	-	-	-
[DEAR]	-	-	-	-	-	+
[LOYAL]	-	-	-	-	-	-
[WEAK]	-	-	-	-	-	-
[WELCOME]	-	-	-	-	-	-
[UNWORTHY]	-	-	-	-	-	-
[FAULTLESS]	-	-	-	-	-	-

---

[18] The Middle English Dictionary defines *renk* as "a row through the midst of an army" (URL 10). As no reference to a single person could be found, the term was interpreted as *soldier*.

57

	comly (URL 13)	cosyn (URL 14)	gome (URL 15)	ientyle (URL 16)	noble (URL 17)	schalk (URL 18)
[NOBLE]	-	-	-	+	+	-
[WARRIOR]	-	-	+	-	-	+
[BRAVE]	-	-	-	-	-	-
[POWERFUL]	-	-	-	-	-	-
[HANDSOME]	+	-	-	-	-	-
[POLITE]	-	-	-	+	-	-
[GOOD]	-	-	-	-	-	-
[STRONG]	-	-	-	-	-	-
[CHEERFUL]	-	-	-	-	-	-
[KIND]	-	-	-	+	-	-
[RELATIVE]	-	+	-	-	-	-
[DEAR]	-	-	-	-	-	-
[WEAK]	-	-	-	-	-	-
[LOYAL]	-	-	-	-	-	-
[WELCOME]	-	-	-	-	-	-
[UNWORTHY]	-	-	-	-	-	-
[FAULTLESS]	-	-	-	-	-	-

	stalworth (URL 19)	tulk (URL 20)	wlonk (URL 21)	wok (URL 22)	sistersun
[NOBLE]	-	-	+	-	-
[WARRIOR]	-	+	-	-	-
[BRAVE]	+	-	+	-	-
[POWERFUL]	-	-	-	-	-
[HANDSOME]	-	-	-	-	-
[POLITE]	-	-	-	-	-
[GOOD]	-	-	-	-	-
[STRONG]	+	-	-	-	-
[CHEERFUL]	-	-	-	-	-
[KIND]	-	-	-	-	-
[RELATIVE]	-	-	-	-	+
[DEAR]	-	-	-	-	-
[WEAK]	-	-	-	+	-
[LOYAL]	-	-	-	-	-
[WELCOME]	-	-	-	-	-
[UNWORTHY]	-	-	-	-	-
[FAULTLESS]	-	-	-	-	-

Table 7 - Semantic Features of Adjectives in *Sir Gawain and the Green Knight*

	gode (URL 23)	bolde (URL 24)	comli (URL 13)	fre (URL 25)	gentyle (URL 16)	hende (URL 11)
[NOBLE]	-	+	-	+	+	+
[WARRIOR]	-	-	-	-	-	-
[BRAVE]	-	+	-	-	-	+
[POWERFUL]	-	-	-	-	-	+
[HANDSOME]	-	-	+	-	-	-
[POLITE]	-	-	-	-	+	+
[GOOD]	+	-	-	-	-	-
[STRONG]	-	-	-	-	-	-
[CHEERFUL]	-	-	-	-	-	-
[KIND]	-	-	-	-	+	-
[RELATIVE]	-	-	-	-	-	-
[DEAR]	-	-	-	-	-	-
[LOYAL]	-	-	-	-	-	-
[WEAK]	-	-	-	-	-	-
[WELCOME]	-	-	-	-	-	-
[UNWORTHY]	-	-	-	-	-	-
[FAULTLESS]	-	-	-	-	-	-

	luflych (URL 26)	stif (URL 27)	derf (URL 28)	fautles (URL 29)	gay (URL 30)	myry (URL 31)
[NOBLE]	-	-	+	-	-	-
[WARRIOR]	-	-	-	-	-	-
[BRAVE]	-	-	+	-	-	-
[POWERFUL]	-	+	+	-	-	-
[HANDSOME]	+	-	-	-	-	-
[POLITE]	-	-	-	-	-	-
[GOOD]	-	-	-	-	-	-
[STRONG]	-	+	+	-	-	-
[CHEERFUL]	-	-	-	-	+	+
[KIND]	-	-	-	-	-	-
[RELATIVE]	-	-	-	-	-	-
[DEAR]	-	-	-	-	-	-
[WEAK]	-	-	-	-	-	-
[LOYAL]	-	-	-	-	-	-
[WELCOME]	-	-	-	-	-	-
[UNWORTHY]	-	-	-	-	-	-
[FAULTLESS]	-	-	-	+	-	-

	noble (URL 32)	siker (URL 33)	trwe (URL 34)	welcome (URL 35)	vnworþy (URL 36)
[NOBLE]	+	-	-	-	-
[WARRIOR]	-	-	-	-	-
[BRAVE]	+	+	-	-	-
[POWERFUL]	-	-	-	-	-
[HANDSOME]	-	-	-	-	-
[POLITE]	-	-	-	-	-
[GOOD]	-	-	-	-	-
[STRONG]	-	-	-	-	-
[CHEERFUL]	-	-	-	-	-
[KIND]	-	-	-	-	-
[RELATIVE]	-	-	-	-	-
[DEAR]	-	-	-	-	-
[WEAK]	-	-	-	-	-
[LOYAL]	-	-	+	-	-
[WELCOME]	-	-	-	+	-
[UNWORTHY]	-	-	-	-	+
[FAULTLESS]	-	-	-	-	-

Table 8 - Semantic Features of Appositions in *Sir Gawain and the Green Knight*

	gode (URL 23)	blyþe (URL 37)	hende (URL 11)	noble (URL 32)
[NOBLE]	-	-	+	+
[WARRIOR]	-	-	-	-
[BRAVE]	-	-	+	+
[POWERFUL]	-	-	+	-
[HANDSOME]	-	-	-	-
[POLITE]	-	-	+	-
[GOOD]	+	-	-	-
[STRONG]	-	-	-	-
[CHEERFUL]	-	+	-	-
[KIND]	-	-	-	-
[RELATIVE]	-	-	-	-
[DEAR]	-	-	-	-
[WEAK]	-	-	-	-
[LOYAL]	-	-	-	-
[WELCOME]	-	-	-	-
[UNWORTHY]	-	-	-	-
[FAULTLESS]	-	-	-	-

III. Complete Data for *Parzival*

Table 9 - Collection of Nouns for *Parzival*

0	Word/Phrase	Note	Verse Line	User
1	âmîs		728,02	N
2	arzet		516,30	O (Orgelûse)
3	arzet		531,15	O (Orgelûse)
4	arzet		523,08	O (Orgelûse)
5	bote		608,01	G
6	bote		380,11	N
7	bruoder		697,07	O (Bêne)
8	bruoder		710,28	O (Itonjê)
9	bruoder		710,11	N
10	bruoder		323,02	N
11	bruoder		323,13	N
12	bruoder		686,07	N
13	bruoder		694,11	N
14	bruoder		686,14	N
15	bruoder		719,27	O (Artûs)
16	bruoder		323,16	O (Bêâcurs)
17	bruoder		711,18	O (Itonjê)
18	bruoder		711,23	O (Itonjê)
19	bruodersun		406,15	G
20	degen		299,30	N
21	degen		339,15	N
22	degen		418,03	N
23	degen		503,20	N
24	degen		534,11	N
25	degen		535,08	N
26	degen		541,12	N
27	degen		666,17	N
28	degen		688,15	N
29	degen		601,14	N
30	degen		432,24	N
31	degen		427,21	O (Antikonîe)
32	degen		602,14	N
33	degene		397,25	N
34	ellens rîche		614,11	O (Orgelûse)
35	êren rîche		581,01	N
36	fil li roi Lôt		341,11	N
37	gans		515,13	O (Orgelûse)
38	garzun		523,09	O (Orgelûse)
39	gast	'stranger'	340,22	G
40	gast	'stranger'	364,28	N
41	gast	'stranger'	398,30	N
42	gast	'guest'	405,23	N

43	gast	'guest'	422,21	N
44	gast	'stranger'	522,17	N
45	gast	'stranger'	572,05	N
46	gast	'guest'	412,19	O
47	gast	'guest'	374,23	O (Obilôt's mother)
48	gast	'stranger'	361,27	O (Scherules)
49	gaste	'guest'	372,03	N
50	gaste	'guest'	410,19	N
51	gaste	'stranger'	368,22	N
52	gaste	'stranger'	530,26	N
53	gaste	'guest'	557,24	N
54	gaste	'guest'	558,14	N
55	gaste	'guest'	553,29	N
56	gaste	'stranger'	601,07	N
57	gastes	'guest'	415,06	O (Antikonîe)
58	gastes	'guest'	363,24	O (Scherules)
59	geselle		516,29	O (Orgelûse)
60	geselle	'beloved'	620,08	O (Orgelûse)
61	gesellen	'beloved'	516,01	O (Orgelûse)
62	gesellen	'friend'	422,14	O (Vergulaht)
63	gesellen		410,05	N
64	helde		541,29	N
65	heldes		426,11	N
66	helt		567,28	N
67	helt		574,28	N
68	helt		582,08	N
69	helt		339,21	N
70	helt		335,17	N
71	helt		342,04	N
72	helt		611,17	N
73	helt		397,29	N
74	helt		578,23	O (Arnîve)
75	helt		581,12	O (Arnîve)
76	helt		581,19	O (Arnîve)
77	helt		411,19	O (Kingrimursel)
78	koufman		361,1	O (Obie)
79	koufman		352,16	O (Obie)
80	lasters arm		581,01	N
81	Lôtes kinde		401,27	N
82	Lôtes kinde		676,08	N
83	Lôtes kint		625,14	N
84	Lôtes kint		351,14	N
85	Lôtes sun		707,15	N
86	Lôtes sun		709,19	N
87	Lôtes sun		543,09	N
88	Lôtes sun		546,26	N
89	Lôtes sun		597,26	N

90	Lôtes sun		300,23	N
91	Lôtes sun		353,02	N
92	Lôtes sun		368,03	N
93	Lôtes sun		387,09	N
94	Lôtes sun		422,29	N
95	Lôtes sun		609,01	N
96	man		607,24	G
97	man		412,07	N
98	man		430,20	N
99	man		512,19	N
100	man		602,24	N
101	man		615,15	N
102	man		621,19	N
103	man		646,18	N
104	man		677,24	N
105	man		756,22	N
106	man		335,02	N
107	man		365,23	N
108	man		584,23	N
109	man		513,02	N
110	man		299,13	N
111	man		513,13	O
112	man		520,19	O (Malcrêâtiure)
113	man		522,07	O (injured knight)
114	man		417,17	O (Kingrimursel)
115	man		374,18	O (Lippaôt)
116	man		374,22	O (Obilôt's mother)
117	man		423,02	N
118	manlîche		331,23	N
119	manne		573,20	N
120	mannen		412,05	O (Vergulaht)
121	meister		405,06	O (Antikonîe)
122	minne gernde		530,15	N
123	neve		672,23	O (Artûs)
124	neve		677,08	O (Artûs)
125	neve		672,23	O (Artûs)
126	neve		650,16	O (Artûs)
127	neve		785,05	O (Feirefîz)
128	neve		693,07	O (Parzivâl)
129	neve		689,22	O (Parzivâl)
130	neve		701,07	O (Parzivâl)
131	neve		701,11	O (Parzivâl)
132	neve		701,17	O (Parzivâl)
133	neven		671,07	N
134	neven		717,19	O (Artûs)
135	neven		719,05	O (Artûs)

136	neven		727,23	N
137	neven		677,06	O (Artûs)
138	neven		672,02	O (Artûs)
139	prîs		301,07	N
140	ritter		620,16	N
141	ritter		361,23	N
142	ritter		574,07	N
143	ritter		574,15	N
144	ritter		620,16	N
145	ritter		414,25	O (Antikonîe)
146	ritter		642,15	O (Arnîve)
147	ritter		368,17	O (Obilôt)
148	ritter		358,02	O (Obilôt)
149	ritter		372,30	O (Obilôt)
150	ritter		373,19	O (Obilôt)
151	ritter		396,06	O (Obilôt)
152	ritter		516,30	O (Orgelûse)
153	ritter		523,06	O (Orgelûse)
154	stolzen		705,11	N
155	sun		66,15	N
156	swester sun		221,07	N
157	swester sun		649,13	O (Artûs)
158	swester sun		726,11	O (Artûs)
159	swester sun		727,10	O (Artûs)
160	swester sun		322,15	O (Artûs)
161	swester sun		298,15	O (Keie)
162	swester sun		684,03	O (Messenger)
163	swestersun		416,06	N
164	trügenære		363,24	O (Lippaôt)
165	tumbe		530,1	O (Orgelûse)
166	valschære		363,16	O (Lippaôt)
167	valschære		362,24	O (Obîe)
168	vriundes		706,23	N
169	vriunt		408,05	N
170	wehselære		353,26	O (Obîe)
171	werde		516,25	N
172	wîgant		553,03	N
173	wîgant		588,11	N
174	wîgant		602,27	N
175	wirt		642,03	N
176	wirt		641,11	N
177	wirt		774,09	N
178	wirte		639,13	N
179	wirte		641,08	N
180	zil		582,2	O (Arnive)

Table 10 - Collection of Adjectives for *Parzival*

	Word/Phrase	Verse Line	User
1	ahtbæren	516,01	O (Orgelûse)
2	balt	397,25	N
3	balt	534,11	N
4	balt	601,14	N
5	balt	339,15	N
6	edeln	530,26	N
7	ellens rîche	331,24	N
8	ellens rîche	418,23	N
9	ellenthafte	418,03	N
10	getriuwer	522,07	O (injured knight)
11	gezimieret	513,02	N
12	guoter	374,22	O (Obilôt's mother)
13	h[ö]vesch	677,24	N
14	hœster	301,07	N
15	hövesch	430,20	N
16	hövesche	756,22	N
17	kamphbære	335,02	N
18	lieber	701,17	O (Parzivâl)
19	manlîch	677,24	N
20	manlîch	430,20	N
21	milten	666,08	N
22	minne gernde	512,19	N
23	minne gernde	615,15	N
24	snel	503,20	N
25	snel	535,08	N
26	starke	602,24	N
27	stolze	403,04	N
28	stolze	599,25	N
29	süezer	374,22	O (Obilôt's mother)
30	triuwen	521,21	N
31	tummer	520,19	O (Malcrêâtiure)
32	unverzaget	426,11	N
33	unverzaget	582,08	N
34	vremden	374,23	O (Obilôt's mother)
35	vremden	368,17	O (Obilôt)
36	vremden	373,19	O (Obilôt)
37	werde	688,15	N
38	werde	339,15	N
39	werde	340,23	N
40	werde	366,19	N
41	werde	371,17	N
42	werde	599,25	N
43	werde	392,17	N
44	werde	394,19	N

45	werde	402,14	N
46	werde	406,12	N
47	werde	624,21	N
48	werde	631,07	N
49	werde	652,05	N
50	werde	668,26	N
51	werde	677,23	N
52	werde	685,06	N
53	werde	703,19	N
54	werde	684,05	O (messenger)
55	werde	646,18	N
56	werde erkande	338,04	N
57	werden	410,19	N
58	werden	530,26	N
59	werden	366,04	N
60	werden	679,01	N
61	werden	689,03	O (Parzivâl)
62	werden	365,23	N
63	werder	374,18	O (Lippaôt)
64	werlîch	607,24	G
65	werlîchen	584,23	N
66	wert	541,12	N
67	wert	666,17	N
68	wert erkant	686,14	N
69	wol geborn	299,30	N
70	wol geborn	602,14	N
71	wol geborne	405,23	N
72	wol geborne	522,17	N
73	wol gelobete	299,13	N
74	wol gevar	361,23	N

Table 11 - Collection of Appositions for *Parzival*

	Phrase	Verse Line	User
1	Gâwân der prîses erkande	558,01	N
2	Gâwân der sælden rîche	670,21	N
3	Gâwân der ellens rîche	544,22	N
4	Gâwân der ellens rîche	602,12	N
5	Gâwân der ellens rîche	418,23	N
6	Gâwân der kurteis	380,28	N
7	Gâwân der kurtois	619,25	N
8	Gâwân der kurtois	672,25	N
9	Gâwân der reht gemuote	339,01	N
10	Gâwân der valsches vrîe	668,03	N
11	Gâwân der wirt	764,08	N
12	Gâwâne dem ellens rîchen	429,12	N
13	von Norwæge Gâwân	651,10	O (Keie)

IV. Semantic Features in *Parzival*

Table 12 - Semantic Features of Nouns in *Parzival*

	man (URL 38)	gast 'guest' (URL 39)	gast 'stranger' (URL 39)	Lôtes sun/kint (URL 40/41)	neve (URL 42)
[RELATIVE]	-	-	-	+	+
[WARRIOR]	-	-	+	-	-
[NOBLE]	-	-	-	-	-
[COURTLY]	-	-	-	-	-
[RESPECTED]	-	-	-	-	-
[HERO]	-	-	-	-	-
[BRAVE]	-	-	-	-	-
[STRANGER]	-	-	+	-	-
[GUEST]	-	+	-	-	-
[HOST]	-	-	-	-	-
[BELOVED]	-	-	-	-	-
[FRIEND]	-	-	-	-	-
[PROUD]	-	-	-	-	-
[BARBER-SURGEON]	-	-	-	-	-
[LOVE LONGING]	-	-	-	-	-
[GLORIOUS]	-	-	-	-	-
[GRACIOUS]	-	-	-	-	-
[QUICK]	-	-	-	-	-
[UNDISMAYED]	-	-	-	-	-
[LOYAL]	-	-	-	-	-
[DUMB]	-	-	-	-	-
[HANDSOME]	-	-	-	-	-
[NORWEGIAN]	-	-	-	-	-
[MESSENGER]	-	-	-	-	-
[FORGER]	-	-	-	-	-
[TRADER]	-	-	-	-	-
[FAULTLESS]	-	-	-	-	-
[DEFRAUDER]	-	-	-	-	-
[STRONG]	-	-	-	-	-
[DEAR]	-	-	-	-	-
[KIND]	-	-	-	-	-
[GOOD]	-	-	-	-	-
[TEACHER]	-	-	-	-	-
[AIM]	-	-	-	-	-
[MONEY LENDER]	-	-	-	-	-
[SQUIRE]	-	-	-	-	-

	ritter (URL 43)	helt (URL 44)	degen (URL 45/61)	bruoder (URL 46)	swester sun (URL 62)
[RELATIVE]	-	-	-	+	+
[WARRIOR]	+	-	+	-	-
[NOBLE]	-	-	-	-	-
[COURTLY]	-	-	-	-	-
[RESPECTED]	-	-	-	-	-
[HERO]	-	+	+	-	-
[BRAVE]	-	-	+	-	-
[STRANGER]	-	-	-	-	-
[GUEST]	-	-	-	-	-
[HOST]	-	-	-	-	-
[BELOVED]	-	-	-	-	-
[FRIEND]	-	-	-	-	-
[PROUD]	-	-	-	-	-
[BARBER-SURGEON]	-	-	-	-	-
[LOVE LONGING]	-	-	-	-	-
[GLORIOUS]	-	-	-	-	-
[GRACIOUS]	-	-	-	-	-
[QUICK]	-	-	-	-	-
[UNDISMAYED]	-	-	-	-	-
[LOYAL]	-	-	-	-	-
[DUMB]	-	-	-	-	-
[HANDSOME]	-	-	-	-	-
[NORWEGIAN]	-	-	-	-	-
[MESSENGER]	-	-	-	-	-
[FORGER]	-	-	-	-	-
[TRADER]	-	-	-	-	-
[FAULTLESS]	-	-	-	-	-
[DEFRAUDER]	-	-	-	-	-
[STRONG]	-	-	-	-	-
[DEAR]	-	-	-	-	-
[KIND]	-	-	-	-	-
[GOOD]	-	-	-	-	-
[TEACHER]	-	-	-	-	-
[AIM]	-	-	-	-	-
[MONEY LENDER]	-	-	-	-	-
[SQUIRE]	-	-	-	-	-

	geselle 'beloved' (URL 63)	geselle 'friend' (URL 63)	wirt (URL 47)	wîgant (URL 48)	vriunt (URL 49)
[RELATIVE]	-	-	-		-
[WARRIOR]	-	-	-	+	-
[NOBLE]	-	-	-	-	-
[COURTLY]	-	-	-	-	-
[RESPECTED]	-	-	-	-	-
[HERO]	-	-	-	+	-
[BRAVE]	-	-	-	-	-
[STRANGER]	-	-	-	-	-
[GUEST]	-	-	-	-	-
[HOST]	-	-	+	-	-
[BELOVED]	+	-	-	-	-
[FRIEND]	-	+	-	-	+
[PROUD]	-	-	-	-	-
[BARBER-SURGEON]	-	-	-	-	-
[LOVE LONGING]	-	-	-	-	-
[GLORIOUS]	-	-	-	-	-
[GRACIOUS]	-	-	-	-	-
[QUICK]	-	-	-	-	-
[UNDISMAYED]	-	-	-	-	-
[LOYAL]	-	-	-	-	-
[DUMB]	-	-	-	-	-
[HANDSOME]	-	-	-	-	-
[NORWEGIAN]	-	-	-	-	-
[MESSENGER]	-	-	-	-	-
[FORGER]	-	-	-	-	-
[TRADER]	-	-	-	-	-
[FAULTLESS]	-	-	-	-	-
[DEFRAUDER]	-	-	-	-	-
[STRONG]	-	-	-	-	-
[DEAR]	-	-	-	-	-
[KIND]	-	-	-	-	-
[GOOD]	-	-	-	-	-
[TEACHER]	-	-	-	-	-
[AIM]	-	-	-	-	-
[MONEY LENDER]	-	-	-	-	-
[SQUIRE]	-	-	-	-	-

	bote (URL 50)	amîs (URL 51)	stolze (URL 52)	werde (URL 53)	minne gernde (URL 54)
[RELATIVE]	-	-	-	-	-
[WARRIOR]	-	-	-	-	-
[NOBLE]	-	-	-	+	-
[COURTLY]	-	-	-	+	-
[RESPECTED]	-	-	-	+	-
[HERO]	-	-	-	-	-
[BRAVE]	-	-	-	-	-
[STRANGER]	-	-	-	-	-
[GUEST]	-	-	-	-	-
[HOST]	-	-	-	-	-
[BELOVED]	-	+	-	-	-
[FRIEND]	-	-	-	-	-
[PROUD]	-	-	+	-	-
[BARBER-SURGEON]	-	-	-	-	-
[LOVE LONGING]	-	-	-	-	+
[GLORIOUS]	-	-	-	-	-
[GRACIOUS]	-	-	-	-	-
[QUICK]	-	-	-	-	-
[UNDISMAYED]	-	-	-	-	-
[LOYAL]	-	-	-	-	-
[DUMB]	-	-	-	-	-
[HANDSOME]	-	-	-	-	-
[NORWEGIAN]	-	-	-	-	-
[MESSENGER]	+	-	-	-	-
[FORGER]	-	-	-	-	-
[TRADER]	-	-	-	-	-
[FAULTLESS]	-	-	-	-	-
[DEFRAUDER]	-	-	-	-	-
[STRONG]	-	-	-	-	-
[DEAR]	-	-	-	-	-
[KIND]	-	-	-	-	-
[GOOD]	-	-	-	-	-
[TEACHER]	-	-	-	-	-
[AIM]	-	-	-	-	-
[MONEY LENDER]	-	-	-	-	-
[SQUIRE]	-	-	-	-	-

	manlîche (URL 55)	ellens rîche (URL 56)	êren rîche (URL 57)	lasters arm (URL 58)	arzet (URL 64)
[RELATIVE]	-	-	-	-	-
[WARRIOR]	-	-	-	-	-
[NOBLE]	-	-	-	-	-
[COURTLY]	-	-	-	-	-
[RESPECTED]	-	-	-	-	-
[HERO]	-	-	-	-	-
[BRAVE]	+	+	-	-	-
[STRANGER]	-	-	-	-	-
[GUEST]	-	-	-	-	-
[HOST]	-	-	-	-	-
[BELOVED]	-	-	-	-	-
[FRIEND]	-	-	-	-	-
[PROUD]	-	-	-	-	-
[BARBER-SURGEON]	-	-	-	-	+
[LOVE LONGING]	-	-	-	-	-
[GLORIOUS]	-	-	+	-	-
[GRACIOUS]	-	-	-	-	-
[QUICK]	-	-	-	-	-
[UNDISMAYED]	-	-	-	-	-
[LOYAL]	-	-	-	-	-
[DUMB]	-	-	-	-	-
[HANDSOME]	-	-	-	-	-
[NORWEGIAN]	-	-	-	-	-
[MESSENGER]	-	-	-	-	-
[FORGER]	-	-	-	-	-
[TRADER]	-	-	-	-	-
[FAULTLESS]	-	-	-	+	-
[DEFRAUDER]	-	-	-	-	-
[STRONG]	-	-	-	-	-
[DEAR]	-	-	-	-	-
[KIND]	-	-	-	-	-
[GOOD]	-	-	-	-	-
[TEACHER]	-	-	-	-	-
[AIM]	-	-	-	-	-
[MONEY LENDER]	-	-	-	-	-
[SQUIRE]	-	-	-	-	-

	koufman (URL 65)	garzun (URL 66)	trügenære (URL 67)	valschære (URL 68)	wehselære (URL 69)
[RELATIVE]	-	-	-	-	-
[WARRIOR]	-	-	-	-	-
[NOBLE]	-	-	-	-	-
[COURTLY]	-	-	-	-	-
[RESPECTED]	-	-	-	-	-
[HERO]	-	-	-	-	-
[BRAVE]	-	-	-	-	-
[STRANGER]	-	-	-	-	-
[GUEST]	-	-	-	-	-
[HOST]	-	-	-	-	-
[BELOVED]	-	-	-	-	-
[FRIEND]	-	-	-	-	-
[PROUD]	-	-	-	-	-
[BARBER-SURGEON]	-	-	-	-	-
[LOVE LONGING]	-	-	-	-	-
[GLORIOUS]	-	-	-	-	-
[GRACIOUS]	-	-	-	-	-
[QUICK]	-	-	-	-	-
[UNDISMAYED]	-	-	-	-	-
[LOYAL]	-	-	-	-	-
[DUMB]	-	-	-	-	-
[HANDSOME]	-	-	-	-	-
[NORWEGIAN]	-	-	-	-	-
[MESSENGER]	-	-	-	-	-
[FORGER]	-	-	-	+	-
[TRADER]	+	-	-	-	-
[FAULTLESS]	-	-	-	-	-
[DEFRAUDER]	-	-	+	-	-
[STRONG]	-	-	-	-	-
[DEAR]	-	-	-	-	-
[KIND]	-	-	-	-	-
[GOOD]	-	-	-	-	-
[TEACHER]	-	-	-	-	-
[AIM]	-	-	-	-	-
[MONEY LENDER]	-	-	-	-	+
[SQUIRE]	-	+	-	-	-

	tumbe (URL 70)	prîs (URL 59)	meister (URL 71)	zil	bruodersun (URL 95)
[RELATIVE]	-	-	-	-	+
[WARRIOR]	-	-	-	-	-
[NOBLE]	-	-	-	-	-
[COURTLY]	-	-	-	-	-
[RESPECTED]	-	-	-	-	-
[HERO]	-	-	-	-	-
[BRAVE]	-	-	-	-	-
[STRANGER]	-	-	-	-	-
[GUEST]	-	-	-	-	-
[HOST]	-	-	-	-	-
[BELOVED]	-	-	-	-	-
[FRIEND]	-	-	-	-	-
[PROUD]	-	-	-	-	-
[BARBER-SURGEON]	-	-	-	-	-
[LOVE LONGING]	-	-	-	-	-
[GLORIOUS]	-	+	-	-	-
[GRACIOUS]	-	-	-	-	-
[QUICK]	-	-	-	-	-
[UNDISMAYED]	-	-	-	-	-
[LOYAL]	-	-	-	-	-
[DUMB]	+	-	-	-	-
[HANDSOME]	-	-	-	-	-
[NORWEGIAN]	-	-	-	-	-
[MESSENGER]	-	-	-	-	-
[FORGER]	-	-	-	-	-
[TRADER]	-	-	-	-	-
[FAULTLESS]	-	-	-	-	-
[DEFRAUDER]	-	-	-	-	-
[STRONG]	-	-	-	-	-
[DEAR]	-	-	-	-	-
[KIND]	-	-	-	-	-
[GOOD]	-	-	-	-	-
[TEACHER]	-	-	+	-	-
[AIM]	-	-	-	+	-
[MONEY LENDER]	-	-	-	-	-
[SQUIRE]	-	-	-	-	-

Table 13 - Semantic Features of Adjectives in *Parzival*

	werde (URL 53)	balt (URL 75)	wol geborn (URL 76)	hövesch (URL 77)	vremd (URL 78)
[RELATIVE]	-	-	-	-	-
[WARRIOR]	-	-	-	-	-
[NOBLE]	+	-	+	+	-
[COURTLY]	+	-	-	+	-
[RESPECTED]	+	-	-	-	-
[HERO]	-	-	-	-	-
[BRAVE]	-	+	-	-	-
[STRANGER]	-	-	-	-	+
[GUEST]	-	-	-	-	-
[HOST]	-	-	-	-	-
[BELOVED]	-	-	-	-	-
[FRIEND]	-	-	-	-	-
[PROUD]	-	-	-	-	-
[BARBER-SURGEON]	-	-	-	-	-
[LOVE LONGING]	-	-	-	-	-
[GLORIOUS]	-	-	-	-	-
[GRACIOUS]	-	-	-	-	-
[QUICK]	-	-	-	-	-
[UNDISMAYED]	-	-	-	-	-
[LOYAL]	-	-	-	-	-
[DUMB]	-	-	-	-	-
[HANDSOME]	-	-	-	-	-
[NORWEGIAN]	-	-	-	-	-
[MESSENGER]	-	-	-	-	-
[FORGER]	-	-	-	-	-
[TRADER]	-	-	-	-	-
[FAULTLESS]	-	-	-	-	-
[DEFRAUDER]	-	-	-	-	-
[STRONG]	-	-	-	-	-
[DEAR]	-	-	-	-	-
[KIND]	-	-	-	-	-
[GOOD]	-	-	-	-	-
[TEACHER]	-	-	-	-	-
[AIM]	-	-	-	-	-
[MONEY LENDER]	-	-	-	-	-
[SQUIRE]	-	-	-	-	-

	ellens rîche (URL 56)	manlîch (URL 55)	snel (URL 79)	stolze (URL 52)	unverzaget (URL 80)
[RELATIVE]	-	-	-	-	-
[WARRIOR]	-	-	-	-	-
[NOBLE]	-	-	-	-	-
[COURTLY]	-	-	-	-	-
[RESPECTED]	-	-	-	-	-
[HERO]	-	-	-	-	-
[BRAVE]	+	+	-	-	-
[STRANGER]	-	-	-	-	-
[GUEST]	-	-	-	-	-
[HOST]	-	-	-	-	-
[BELOVED]	-	-	-	-	-
[FRIEND]	-	-	-	-	-
[PROUD]	-	-	-	+	-
[BARBER-SURGEON]	-	-	-	-	-
[LOVE LONGING]	-	-	-	-	-
[GLORIOUS]	-	-	-	-	-
[GRACIOUS]	-	-	-	-	-
[QUICK]	-	-	+	-	-
[UNDISMAYED]	-	-	-	-	+
[LOYAL]	-	-	-	-	-
[DUMB]	-	-	-	-	-
[HANDSOME]	-	-	-	-	-
[NORWEGIAN]	-	-	-	-	-
[MESSENGER]	-	-	-	-	-
[FORGER]	-	-	-	-	-
[TRADER]	-	-	-	-	-
[FAULTLESS]	-	-	-	-	-
[DEFRAUDER]	-	-	-	-	-
[STRONG]	-	-	-	-	-
[DEAR]	-	-	-	-	-
[KIND]	-	-	-	-	-
[GOOD]	-	-	-	-	-
[TEACHER]	-	-	-	-	-
[AIM]	-	-	-	-	-
[MONEY LENDER]	-	-	-	-	-
[SQUIRE]	-	-	-	-	-

	werlîch (URL 81)	(ge)triuwe (URL 82)	minne gernde (URL 54)	ahtbære (URL 83)	edel (URL 84)
[RELATIVE]	-	-	-	-	-
[WARRIOR]	+	-	-	-	
[NOBLE]	-	-	-	-	+
[COURTLY]	-	-	-	-	-
[RESPECTED]	-	-	-	+	-
[HERO]	-	-	-	-	-
[BRAVE]	+	-	-	-	-
[STRANGER]	-	-	-	-	-
[GUEST]	-	-	-	-	-
[HOST]	-	-	-	-	-
[BELOVED]	-	-	-	-	-
[FRIEND]	-	-	-	-	-
[PROUD]	-	-	-	-	-
[BARBER-SURGEON]	-	-	-	-	-
[LOVE LONGING]	-	-	+	-	-
[GLORIOUS]	-	-	-	-	-
[GRACIOUS]	-	-	-	-	-
[QUICK]	-	-	-	-	-
[UNDISMAYED]	-	-	-	-	-
[LOYAL]	-	+	-	-	-
[DUMB]	-	-	-	-	-
[HANDSOME]	-	-	-	-	-
[NORWEGIAN]	-	-	-	-	-
[MESSENGER]	-	-	-	-	-
[FORGER]	-	-	-	-	-
[TRADER]	-	-	-	-	-
[FAULTLESS]	-	-	-	-	-
[DEFRAUDER]	-	-	-	-	-
[STRONG]	-	-	-	-	-
[DEAR]	-	-	-	-	-
[KIND]	-	-	-	-	-
[GOOD]	-	-	-	-	-
[TEACHER]	-	-	-	-	-
[AIM]	-	-	-	-	-
[MONEY LENDER]	-	-	-	-	-
[SQUIRE]	-	-	-	-	-

	ellenthaft (URL 85)	kamphbære (URL 86)	milte (URL 87)	starc (URL 88)	tumm (URL 89)
[RELATIVE]	-	-	-	-	-
[WARRIOR]	-	+	-	-	-
[NOBLE]	-	-	-	-	-
[COURTLY]	-	-	-	-	-
[RESPECTED]	-	-	-	-	-
[HERO]	-	-	-	-	-
[BRAVE]	+	-	-	-	-
[STRANGER]	-	-	-	-	-
[GUEST]	-	-	-	-	-
[HOST]	-	-	-	-	-
[BELOVED]	-	-	-	-	-
[FRIEND]	-	-	-	-	-
[PROUD]	-	-	-	-	-
[BARBER-SURGEON]	-	-	-	-	-
[LOVE LONGING]	-	-	-	-	-
[GLORIOUS]	-	-	-	-	-
[GRACIOUS]	-	-	-	-	-
[QUICK]	-	-	-	-	-
[UNDISMAYED]	-	-	-	-	-
[LOYAL]	-	-	-	-	-
[DUMB]	-	-	-	-	+
[HANDSOME]	-	-	-	-	-
[NORWEGIAN]	-	-	-	-	-
[MESSENGER]	-	-	-	-	-
[FORGER]	-	-	-	-	-
[TRADER]	-	-	-	-	-
[FAULTLESS]	-	-	-	-	-
[DEFRAUDER]	-	-	-	-	-
[STRONG]	-	-	-	+	-
[DEAR]	-	-	-	-	-
[KIND]	-	-	-	-	-
[GOOD]	-	-	-	-	-
[TEACHER]	-	-	-	-	-
[AIM]	-	-	-	-	-
[MONEY LENDER]	-	-	-	-	-
[SQUIRE]	-	-	-	-	-

	liep (URL 90)	gezimieret (URL 91)	süeze (URL 92)	wol gelobet	wol gevar (URL 93)	vil gouter (URL 94)
[RELATIVE]	-	-	-	-	-	-
[WARRIOR]	-	-	-	-	-	-
[NOBLE]	-	-	-	-	-	-
[COURTLY]	-	-	-	-	-	-
[RESPECTED]	-	-	-	+	-	-
[HERO]	-	-	-	-	-	-
[BRAVE]	-	-	-	-	-	-
[STRANGER]	-	-	-	-	-	-
[GUEST]	-	-	-	-	-	-
[HOST]	-	-	-	-	-	-
[BELOVED]	-	-	-	-	-	-
[FRIEND]	-	-	-	-	-	-
[PROUD]	-	-	-	-	-	-
[BARBER-SURGEON]	-	-	-	-	-	-
[LOVE LONGING]	-	-	-	-	-	-
[GLORIOUS]	-	-	-	-	-	-
[GRACIOUS]	-	-	-	-	-	-
[QUICK]	-	-	-	-	-	-
[UNDISMAYED]	-	-	-	-	-	-
[LOYAL]	-	-	-	-	-	-
[DUMB]	-	-	-	-	-	-
[HANDSOME]	-	+	-	-	+	-
[NORWEGIAN]	-	-	-	-	-	-
[MESSENGER]	-	-	-	-	-	-
[FORGER]	-	-	-	-	-	-
[TRADER]	-	-	-	-	-	-
[FAULTLESS]	-	-	-	-	-	-
[DEFRAUDER]	-	-	-	-	-	-
[STRONG]	-	-	-	-	-	-
[DEAR]	+	-	-	-	-	-
[KIND]	-	-	+	-	-	-
[GOOD]	-	-	-	-	-	+
[TEACHER]	-	-	-	-	-	-
[AIM]	-	-	-	-	-	-
[MONEY LENDER]	-	-	-	-	-	-
[SQUIRE]	-	-	-	-	-	-

Table 14 - Semantic Features of Appositions in *Parzival*

	ellens rîche (URL 56)	kurtois (URL 72)	wirt (URL 47)	prîs (URL 59)
[RELATIVE]	-	-	-	-
[WARRIOR]	-	-	-	-
[NOBLE]	-	-	-	-
[COURTLY]	-	+		
[RESPECTED]	-	-	-	-
[HERO]	-	-	-	-
[BRAVE]	+	-	-	-
[STRANGER]	-	-	-	-
[GUEST]	-	-	-	-
[HOST]	-	-	+	-
[BELOVED]	-	-	-	-
[FRIEND]	-	-	-	-
[PROUD]	-	-	-	-
[BARBER-SURGEON]	-	-	-	-
[LOVE LONGING]	-	-	-	-
[GLORIOUS]	-	-	-	+
[GRACIOUS]	-	-	-	-
[QUICK]	-	-	-	-
[UNDISMAYED]	-	-	-	-
[LOYAL]	-	-	-	-
[DUMB]	-	-	-	-
[HANDSOME]	-	-	-	-
[NORWEGIAN]	-	-	-	-
[MESSENGER]	-	-	-	-
[FORGER]	-	-	-	-
[TRADER]	-	-	-	-
[FAULTLESS]	-	-	-	-
[DEFRAUDER]	-	-	-	-
[STRONG]	-	-	-	-
[DEAR]	-	-	-	-
[KIND]	-	-	-	-
[GOOD]	-	-	-	-
[TEACHER]	-	-	-	-
[AIM]	-	-	-	-
[MONEY LENDER]	-	-	-	-
[SQUIRE]	-	-	-	-

	sælden rîche (URL 73)	reht gemuote (URL 74)	valsches vrîe	von Norwæge
[RELATIVE]	-	-	-	-
[WARRIOR]	-	-	-	-
[NOBLE]	-	-	-	-
[COURTLY]	-	+	-	-
[RESPECTED]	-	-	-	-
[HERO]	-	-	-	-
[BRAVE]	-	-	-	-
[STRANGER]	-	-	-	-
[GUEST]	-	-	-	-
[HOST]	-	-	-	-
[BELOVED]	-	-	-	-
[FRIEND]	-	-	-	-
[PROUD]	-	-	-	-
[BARBER-SURGEON]	-	-	-	-
[LOVE LONGING]	-	-	-	-
[GLORIOUS]	-	-	-	-
[GRACIOUS]	+	-	-	-
[QUICK]	-	-	-	-
[UNDISMAYED]	-	-	-	-
[LOYAL]	-	-	-	-
[DUMB]	-	-	-	-
[HANDSOME]	-	-	-	-
[NORWEGIAN]	-	-	-	+
[MESSENGER]	-	-	-	-
[FORGER]	-	-	-	-
[TRADER]	-	-	-	-
[FAULTLESS]	-	-	+	-
[DEFRAUDER]	-	-	-	-
[STRONG]	-	-	-	-
[DEAR]	-	-	-	-
[KIND]	-	-	-	-
[GOOD]	-	-	-	-
[TEACHER]	-	-	-	-
[AIM]	-	-	-	-
[MONEY LENDER]	-	-	-	-
[SQUIRE]	-	-	-	-

V. Comparison of Semantic Features

Figure 5 - Distribution of Semantic Features in Percent

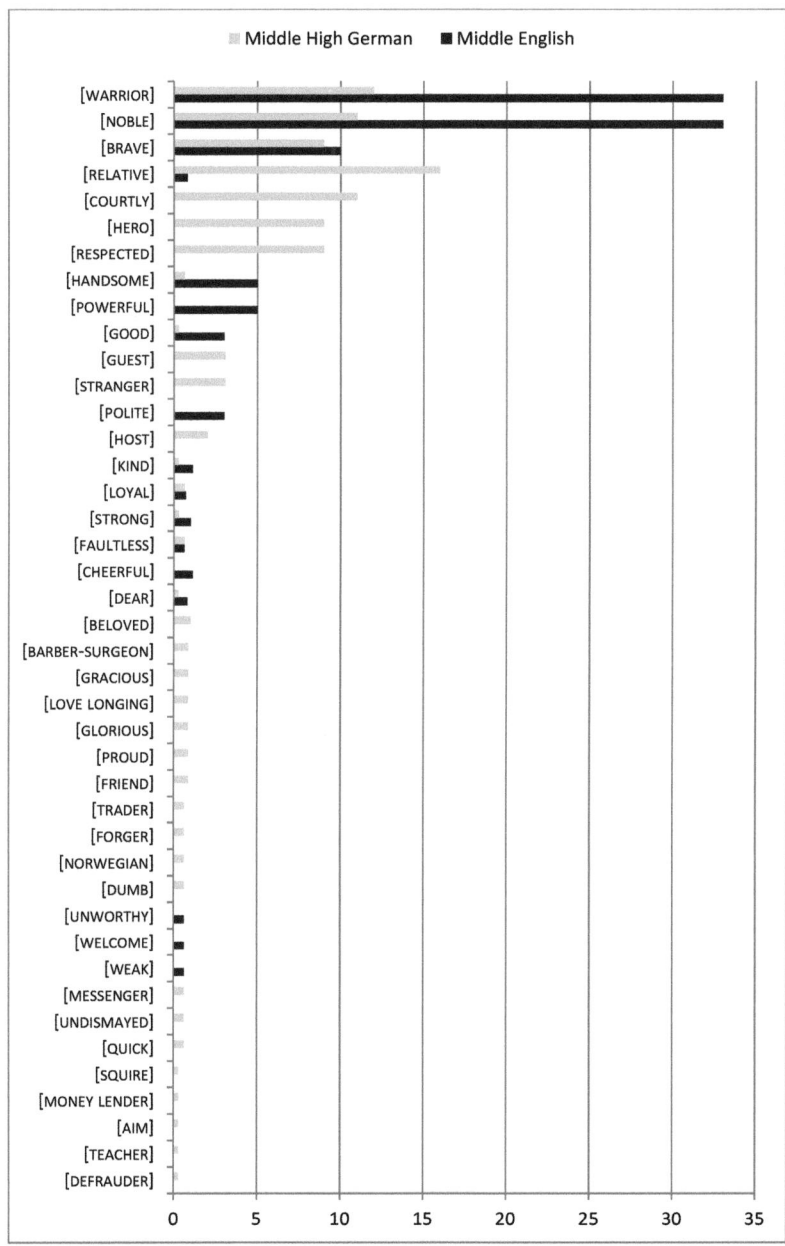